For Basil,

The future we make will be yours. I hope this helps to make it just a little better.

Who's in the Copilot's Seat?

The Ultimate Guide for Small Business Leaders in the Age of AI

NICK DECOURCY

Published by Bright Ideas Agency LLC, Cincinnati, Ohio
(www.brightideasagency.com)

Copyright © 2023 Nick DeCourcy

All rights reserved.

ISBN 979-8-9889994-0-9 (eBook)

ISBN 979-8-9889994-1-6 (Paperback)

Contents

Introduction: The Dawn of AI in Business 1
1. AI and You: The New Business Landscape 5
2. Understanding AI: Basics for Business Leaders 11
3. The Productivity Benefits of a Copilot 18
4. Strategic Considerations for AI in Business 29
5. Leadership in the Age of AI: Guiding Your Team Forward 41
6. Planning Tools and Approaches: Understanding and analyzing your processes 47
7. Preparing Your Workforce: HR Strategies for the AI Era 58
8. AI and Privacy: Navigating Legal and Ethical Considerations 72
9. The Role of AI in Decision-Making and Data Analysis 80
10. Leveraging AI for Customer Service and Marketing 92
11. AI and Operations: Streamlining Business Processes 100
12. AI Risk Management: Mitigating Potential Pitfalls 105
13. Microsoft's Copiloted Future 110
14. The growing AI arms race: Introducing Bard, Claude, and a cast of thousands. 115
Conclusion: Embracing AI as Your Business Copilot 119
How was AI used in writing this book? 121
Further Reading 123
About the author 131

Introduction: The Dawn of AI in Business

For small and medium businesses, the only constant is change. As business leaders, we have adapted to new technologies, new marketplaces, and new ways of working; each with its own unique set of challenges and opportunities.

Today, we stand on the brink of yet another transformation; the age of Artificial Intelligence (AI).

Unlike some previous changes, the rise of AI isn't predominantly about adopting new tools or methods—it's about fundamentally reshaping the way we think about our businesses, how we run them, and how we engage with our teams and our customers.

The integration of AI into everyday business practices marks a significant shift, but it's one that's already underway, and has been for some time. AI is in the background of much of what we do in business and at home. If you use Google Maps to look at a Streetview image of a location, those images have been stitched together with AI. If you browse your Netflix home screen and see a bunch of shows that appeal to you, that content has been selected by AI. If you file an expenses claim at work just by snapping a copy of a receipt and adding it into an app, that image recognition has been powered by AI. The list of existing AI-enabled experiences that happen seamlessly in the background is both long and broad.

If AI has been all around us for a while, what's so different with what's going on now?

In the fall of 2022, the release of ChatGPT from OpenAI caused a revolution. Suddenly, AI broke out of the background and into the cultural zeitgeist as an active participant in our lives. People, with no previous AI expertise or history of technology wizardry, suddenly saw the potential for the automation of repetitive tasks, for providing intelligent insights and recommendations, and for having an AI-based friendly and accessible interface for manipulating our mountains of data.

This was a new type of AI, called generative artificial intelligence, that didn't only do clever data processing with highly specific inputs (such as recognizing a supermarket receipt in your expenses claim), but could work conversationally to grasp the context of natural language prompts provided by a user and generate a unique response.

ChatGPT was quickly followed by Bing Chat from Microsoft, Bard from Google, and an ever-growing assortment of different, if generally more specific, AI tools from major technology companies and startups alike. For many of these tools the business case was obvious, get more done, more quickly, and with reference to more information. Conceptually every type of business and worker could benefit.

Through these rapid changes, Microsoft remained at the forefront of the big technology companies, mainly due to the $1 billion investment (and recently increased dramatically) it had made into OpenAI. It took OpenAI's tooling and its own business application accomplishments and developed the concept of the "AI copilot", a way to infuse the benefits of AI into the tools we use every day while leaving them firmly in the hands of the software's human users. The copilot works as a partner and assistant, rather than as a computer-based replacement. Copilot will be everywhere through Microsoft's product line, from security products to coding tools, and from word processors to image editors.

This book, "Who's in the Copilot's Seat? The Ultimate Guide for Small Business Leaders in the Age of AI," aims to be your guide through this new landscape. It's designed to help you understand what AI is, how it can be used, and what it means for the future of your business. It will help you plan for this new copilot-assisted era, where nearly every worker and business will be able to benefit from AI, but only if you, as the pilot, determine the right flight plan and take off time.

Where technical examples are given, we will mainly focus on Microsoft's productivity suite and its Copilot tools. There are tools with broadly similar capabilities in Google's Workspace product line, and as this book was being finalized, OpenAI announced a more business-focused version of its ChatGPT tool too. As time goes on, we can expect to see AI capabilities growing in terms of range and sophistication across the software products we use every day.

In the following chapters, we'll delve into how you can plan for the impact of AI across your whole business, leveraging it as a differentiator, and understanding how it might bring changes to everything from HR policies to using your intellectual property. We will reflect on the role our AI copilots might take but also consider where other, more specific, technology may need to be deployed to truly maximize your return.

The journey into the age of AI may feel daunting, but remember, every generation of business leaders has faced their own transformative challenges. The goal of this guide is to help you navigate this new era with confidence, harness the power of AI, and ensure your business thrives in the years to come.

So, buckle up, and let's get started—because it's time to get to know the occupant of that copilot's seat!

How to use this book

While many will benefit from reading this book from cover to cover, others with existing knowledge of AI or with specific interests in implementing it in certain functions may benefit more from dipping into chapters that cover those topics or themes.

Each chapter has been given a clear heading so you can understand what topics it explores, and important connecting threads that are relevant in many or all chapters, like the ethics of using AI, are explored in various places from different perspectives.

Many chapters include an **"Action Steps"** section at the end to summarize some of the steps you might take or discussions you might initiate in your business to build out your own, unique, plan for AI adoption.

Use this book as a primer on the whole issue of AI for your business, or as a focused planning aid to ensure you are considering the right issues across different parts of your AI adoption journey.

For topics that are of particular interest to you, or where you wish to follow-up on specific issues that are referenced, resources that were used during the writing of this book and other relevant sources are listed on a chapter-by-chapter basis in the Further Reading section. Be aware that this is a fast-changing subject, and when referring to anything related to specific products, services, or capabilities, you should endeavor to ensure you are looking at the most recent information.

1. AI and You: The New Business Landscape

When we think of Artificial Intelligence (AI), our minds often jump to the futuristic visions of the worst excesses of sci-fi movies. Many of us are quick to jump from a search box that lets us generate interesting content to robots leading a world-wide apocalypse in the style of the Matrix movies or similar. But the reality of AI in today's world—and particularly in the realm of small and medium businesses—is far less about autonomous machines and far more about somewhat intelligent systems that augment human capabilities and drive efficiencies.

Not too long ago, AI tools that could effectively add value through us having conversational interactions with them every day seemed like a concept for the distant future. But that future is now, and not just for high-tech companies or big corporations, but for smaller businesses and individuals. These tools can help us make better decisions and enhance our interactions with customers or colleagues, all while potentially providing us with better balance between our work and personal lives.

Understanding AI in Business

What does this really mean though? How can you approach AI in a way that makes sense and generates benefit? Too often we spend time chasing down the latest trendy app or technology that promises to be a silver-bullet for business performance, and it fizzles out without having any real impact. Why is this different?

The technology revolution that has happened over the last 50 years has had undoubted benefits. However, there is also a darker flip side where we see an ever-growing gap between the potential of new technology and its delivered gains across many businesses and industries. Many of us struggle under mountains of data, constant emails and chats, and an inability to fully disconnect for reflection or focus. These issues have surfaced as discontentment from workers, growing incidence of mental health problems, and mistrust of technology and the companies that lead in its development.

Artificial Intelligence offers a set of tools that can eliminate or reduce those problems at their foundations. There's no reason to sink under a mountain of data when you have AI tools to help you manage it and to gain the right insights from it at the right time. You can allow AI to surface the most important communications to you and keep you up to speed with summaries of long chains, meaning that you don't need to respond to every ping of your phone or PC. And AI can help you take care of mundane or repetitive aspects of your work to give you more time to focus, reflect, and generate ideas that will allow you to improve and grow your business.

The copilot analogy Microsoft has developed for its suite of AI products is an important one for understanding how these tools are designed to work. Bringing AI into your business isn't about replacing humans – it's about supplementing and supporting them, to allow them to add the greatest value, while reducing their focus on low-value tasks that can be frustrating and disengaging. We can make work more productive, while also making it more engaging **and** more balanced.

Like any change in business, what your organization will get out of the AI revolution will be driven by how well you plan, communicate, and execute. Even the most promising technology can fail to have impact with poor change management, and an average product can lead to massive gains if connected with robust cultural realignment to make it fit your use case.

The Anatomy of an AI Chat

For the generative AI tools we will focus on in this book, the primary interface users have to interact with them is a text box where they type a natural language query.

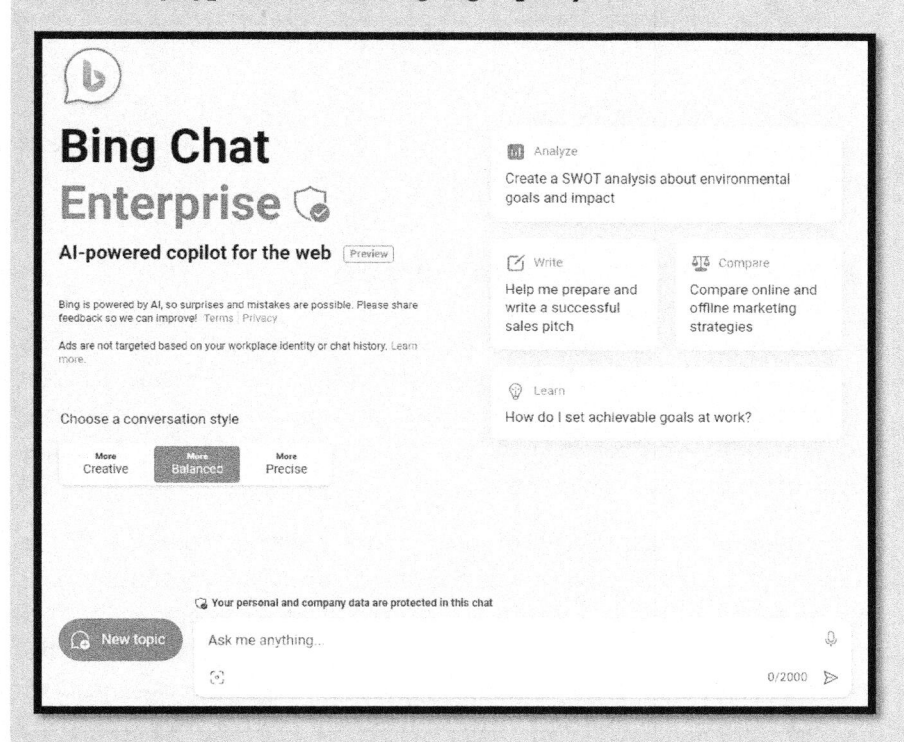

Figure 1: The start screen for Bing Chat Enterprise showing a text box with the direction "Ask me anything..."

This query is referred to as a **prompt** and can be very basic, "What is the time right now in New York?", to something very complex, including lots of directions on how to respond to contextual information or data.

Based on this prompt, the generative AI tool will generate a **response**, often in natural language, but depending on the tool you're using, this could be in a range of formats including tables, graphics, images, videos, or audio. It may also directly generate its response into a file.

Sometimes, either based on the tool in use or the prompt you submitted, the AI tool will respond by asking you follow-up questions or for more data before providing you with its final response. For this reason, these interactions are part of a dialog or chat rather than a single transaction.

In most cases, the chat will be retained in memory so you can continue the discussion and build on the topics already considered. But, depending on the specific tool and tier of license being used, your chat may or may not be saved for future use.

Navigating the AI Landscape

As a business leader, navigating the new AI landscape can seem daunting. It's not just about understanding what AI can do, but also about understanding how it fits into your business strategy, how it affects your team, and how to properly balance the risks and opportunities it presents.

Like any new technology, or really any change, there is not a one-size-fits-all solution for benefiting from AI in your business. You need to fully understand the strengths you are trying to amplify, the weaknesses you are aiming to mitigate, and the external picture of opportunities and threats that are around you. Your implementation of the AI toolset may be very different to other similar businesses based on a few unique challenges you identify.

If you identify that you have a highly engaged team and you've done a good job of building work-life balance, you may focus your AI adoption on tooling for growth while maintaining those other characteristics. Conversely, if you have grown rapidly but your team is struggling to keep pace, and this is leading to disengagement, you might focus on how to use AI tools to automate and eliminate low-value work, to make your teams feel more supported and to re-engage them on aspects of their work where they are more passionate.

Over time you can achieve many goals, but you must start out with a plan that addresses issues that can be quick and impactful wins that allow you and your team to visualize the ongoing benefit these tools can deliver.

One of the big problems with jumping on board with any quickly disrupting technology is separating the wheat from the chaff. There is a wealth of highly specialized AI-powered tools emerging into the market alongside the more generalized frameworks from companies like Microsoft that aim to bring a common "copilot" layer to many of its apps. You might find something that fits your need well, but for reasons we will review throughout this book, this is always going to be a risky path rather than first embracing the AI tooling being added to the familiar products like Outlook and Word that you've been using for decades.

However, as a leader planning for the impact of AI on your business, having a reasonable overview of the market that exists around these technologies is important.

Embrace the Journey, Not the Destination

Gaining value from AI in your business will be a journey. There will be deliverable steps along the way, but it is not about reaching a certain destination immediately. It is about fostering an approach of continuous improvement that embraces the opportunity to enhance systems and processes. It is about promoting a culture of innovation and curiosity, where AI is not seen as a threat, but as a partner, or copilot, in achieving more and achieving better.

Through this guide, we will delve deeper into how to frame this journey and what important stops you might want to plan along the way. A lot of what we consider will focus on people rather than on technology. At its core, AI provides a set of tools that will greatly impact how the people around you spend their time, and how they add value particularly when leveraging other technologies, you are already more familiar with.

Remember, in this new era of AI, you're not alone in the cockpit. You're in the pilot's chair, but AI is your copilot, ready to help you navigate the new business landscape.

Action Steps

- Consider the biases that may exist toward AI from the people around you in your business. Perhaps read some articles looking at negative perspectives around this issue to start to better understand the objections your colleagues may have, both conceptually and specifically within your business.

- Think about the obvious pain points that exist in your organization where a little extra help from basic AI tools might make a difference and start to tell a positive story about this technology.

- Start to paint a mental picture of your AI journey. Why are you reading this book? What stops do you want to make on your flight as you get used to working with an AI copilot?

2. Understanding AI: Basics for Business Leaders

Understanding what AI is, and what it is not, is an essential foundation for starting our journey. For many of us that involves undoing decades of subconscious exposure to fanciful depictions of AI in books, movies, and TV, which are not relevant, and often unhelpful, to our view of the technologies that are starting to be before us today.

It is important to remember that by engaging with this book, you are giving yourself the opportunity to inquire more deeply into this issue and to better understand AI as a concept. Those around you won't necessarily undertake similar homework before expressing their views about any AI journey you start in your business. Being always cognizant of the propensity that exists for negative stereotypes to be at the forefront of our AI conversations will equip you to have better dialogs, no matter those existing biases.

What is Artificial Intelligence (AI)?

Artificial Intelligence, or AI, is a branch of computer science that aims to create systems capable of performing tasks that would normally require, and up until recently have required, human intelligence. This includes tasks such as processing natural language, recognizing patterns, predicting the answer to problems, and learning from experience.

There are two broad categories of AI systems. Narrow AI performs a specific task, such as processing natural language or voice recognition. General AI is not limited by a specific task, and generally can compete with human capabilities across the spectrum of intellectual tasks. Currently, all the AI platforms we have available, including new ones like ChatGPT, are examples of narrow AI.

Because AI systems have narrow but different capabilities, there are a range of flavors of such systems that have been developed to help with different tasks. These systems are built with different components that provide varied capabilities depending on the purpose of the AI system:

Machine Learning (ML): This is the process by which AI systems learn from data, identifying patterns, and making decisions or predictions. For example, ML can take your company's past sales data and use it to make future predictions about what you might sell in each month.

Example: Imagine you run an e-commerce store. ML algorithms can analyze past customer behaviors, items bought, and time spent on each page. Using this data, the algorithm can predict what items a customer is likely to buy next, helping you in targeted marketing.

Natural Language Processing (NLP): This is the technology that allows machines to understand and create human language. NLP is what allows a platform like ChatGPT to understand a human language prompt and deliver information back to you based on it.

Example: NLP technology is behind chat support systems. If one customer types 'What is your return policy?', while another types 'Can I still return my purchase?', the NLP capability understands the intent of both queries is the same and can automatically respond with the appropriate information, reducing the need for human intervention.

Computer Vision: This technology allows computers to see visual information such as images and to understand it. An example of this is automated receipt processing that you see in products such as QuickBooks, where you can upload an image of a receipt and the software works out what the details of the expense are.

> **Example:** In a manufacturing setting, computer vision tools can scan items on a conveyor belt for defects. The system can identify damaged goods and automatically sort them out, ensuring only quality products reach the end customer.

Robotic Process Automation (RPA): This allows the AI tool to automate computer-based actions that are commonly performed by humans, such as entering data, or saving and organizing files. Microsoft Power Automate Desktop is an example of a software used to leverage this type of technology and allows the computer to control your Windows PC. RPA is commonly used to connect and automate processes involving systems that cannot be accessed by other automation technologies, such systems may include old end-of-life software that continues to be used in businesses for certain key functions or custom developed software that was never built with automation in mind. Because RPA allows you to simulate mouse clicks and keyboard entry, practically any software that runs on a supported operating system can be included in automated processes, and often linked to broader automations that include the use of cloud-based technologies too.

> **Example:** RPA can be used in a HR setting to automate the repetitive task of data entry for new employees onboarding into an aging HRIS (Human Resources Information System) tool that doesn't have modern connected web capabilities. The RPA bot will fill in forms, upload documents, and even coordinate scheduling with other systems, freeing up HR team members for more strategic work.

Knowledge Representation and Reasoning (KR&R): Allows the AI tool to use information about the world in a way that allows it to solve complex tasks such as online customer support. Tools such as Microsoft Power Virtual Agents allow you to create chatbots that represent KR&R AI features. This aspect of

AI is increasingly important as the challenge moves from not just completing tightly focused or esoteric tasks, but doing work connected with how human workers experience and interpret the world around them. The ability for AI tools to solve problems in a correct and understandable context is a key facet of products like Microsoft 365 Copilot.

> **Example:** A KR&R system accesses a company's HR policies from the company Intranet to allow an employee to ask a chatbot "How many days of vacation do I get after my fifth year of employment?" without having to find the specific document or read a series of extensive policies.

There are many other more specialized areas of AI and subsets of these fields, and many tools will overlap capabilities from several of these categories. For example, a self-driving car will use computer vision to understand its surroundings, but the decisions it makes while driving will be guided by processes based on machine learning.

Leveraging tools incorporating these AI capabilities has become increasingly easy over time. Through Microsoft's Azure Cognitive Services, you can build tools that have pay-by-consumption as-needed access to many of these resources, and with the recent addition of OpenAI tooling through the Azure OpenAI Service, any developer, on any scale, can get access to the world's best in class AI capabilities. However, for small businesses where custom pro-code development is not an option in many cases, services like Power Platform AI Builder, or Power Virtual Agents, provide access to many AI tools with low-code development options. Amazon Web Services (AWS) and Google Cloud also have products that offer many similar capabilities, but in terms of integration with a low-code business-user focused platform, Microsoft is widely regarded as having the edge with its Power Platform suite of products.

Alongside this development, advancements have been made in crafting AI tools that can better generate information for us to understand how they got to their outputs. This concept is called

Explainable AI or XAI and is a separate field of research. For a function like scanning a receipt, this isn't too important, as we can both see the receipt and the data that was created, but for generative functions where it's unclear how the input drives the output, knowing the intermediate steps can be critical in being able to rely on what is created or suggested. For nearly any type of use case where generative AI is relied upon, XAI concepts are important for transparency and trust.

The Benefits of AI for Small and Medium Businesses

AI offers a wide range of benefits for businesses of all sizes, but for smaller businesses that find ways to engage with these technologies there is a potential significant upside of leveling the playing field against larger enterprises.

As a small team you may be limited in what you can produce, but the capabilities of the AI tools you'll be using will not be limited by your scale, and for any given task using the same data will be able to compete with the capacity even the largest enterprise has to complete that task. This is why AI technology is so exciting and should be particularly a reason for excitement for those leading smaller businesses who are wanting to grow and scale.

Here are a few ways AI can add value to your business:

Improve productivity and efficiency: AI can help you automate repetitive or mundane tasks that don't need human imagination. For example, you can automate the entry of invoices or bills into your accounting system, freeing up your finance professionals to focus on higher-value tasks that add more benefit to your business.

Example: Use AI-based invoice processing to automatically extract and enter bill details into your accounting software. This allows your finance team to spend more time on budget planning and financial analysis.

Putting the data into decision-making: Using AI tools you can analyze large quantities of data quickly and accurately, finding patterns and insights that would be difficult for a human at that scale and in that timeframe. With better reporting that more easily conveys the narrative of your business, it's easier to know what to focus on and what decisions to make.

Example: Utilize an AI analytics tool to analyze customer behavior on your e-commerce website. The tool can highlight which products are most viewed or purchased, helping you make data-driven decisions on inventory and marketing.

Delight your customers: AI can help you respond to your customers' needs quicker and to be responsive outside business hours. Tools like AI powered chatbots can provide customers with an easy interface at any time, but you can integrate AI into practically any touch point you have with those you do business with.

Example: Implement an AI-powered chatbot on your website to handle common customer queries 24/7. This not only enhances customer experience but also frees up your customer support team to handle more complex issues.

Supercharge creativity and innovation: Allow your human workers to maximize the power of their imagination by having your AI workers focus on routine, mundane tasks that only serve to deenergize engagement and creativity. However, AI can even assist you with creative endeavors by helping you to keep on top of the ideas that come out of brainstorming meetings, drafting text, or even undertaking visual design.

Example: Employ AI tools that can assist in drafting promotional materials or initial design sketches based on your team's creative input. This allows your marketing and design teams to focus on fine-tuning and innovation.

Create a better balance for employees: Hiring and retaining the best talent is tough, and there's no single silver bullet solution to this problem. But AI does offer an opportunity to redefine your company's culture around work-life balance by eliminating busywork, automating out-of-hours work requests, and allowing team members to focus most of their time on more highly engaging and fulfilling aspects of work.

> **Example:** Use AI to automate routine after-hours tasks like sending follow-up emails or generating end-of-day reports. This enables your employees to achieve a better work-life balance, potentially increasing job satisfaction and retention.

A tool like Microsoft 365 Copilot provides capabilities that can check off some, but not all, of these potential uses of AI. To deliver everything that AI can achieve will require a broad set of tools, of which a copilot in your productivity apps will be important to certain requirements and certain types of work.

Understanding AI is the first step towards harnessing its potential. In the coming chapters, we will explore how to integrate AI into your business strategy, how to lead your team in the age of AI, and how to manage the technological and human aspects of AI adoption.

Remember, AI is not here to replace what we do with our teams, but to supplement and improve, to enhance productivity, and to help us navigate the growing complexity and connectivity of the business world.

Action Steps

- Review the different types of AI capabilities. Do you already have AI tools in any of these categories deployed in your business? Keep a list of these tools as they are important to maintain context as you communicate your future AI goals.

3. The Productivity Benefits of a Copilot

Around 50% of businesses already use Microsoft Office or Microsoft 365, and most business leaders have at least some familiarity with Microsoft's suite of Office products. The Copilot concept isn't really a new app that sits alongside Word or PowerPoint, but a tool that lives inside Word and PowerPoint (and pretty much every other productivity app), as a connecting AI glue for all Microsoft's suite of products. This is framed as an assistant for the work you would be doing normally, but with capabilities to help you achieve more, and to do so more quickly than ever before.

(If your business uses Google Workspace, which is the other market leader, then don't worry, while some technical examples in this book focus on Microsoft's products and on its Copilot AI tools, Google has rolled out very similar functionality across its suite too. Everything contained in this book about the **why** and **how** of AI will equally apply here, just not the specific product-focused examples).

To be clear, Copilot isn't just going to live inside Office. The flavor of Copilot in your Office apps will be called Microsoft 365 Copilot, but as of the time of writing this section, we already know that the Copilot tool concept will appear elsewhere across Microsoft's products, including SharePoint, Power Apps, Power Automate, as a standalone capability called Microsoft 365 Chat, and even in administrative products such as Security Copilot. If you're a Windows 11 user, you're also going to see Microsoft Copilot in Windows which will help you get things done across the operating system as a whole.

The important point is that Copilot isn't a new app with completely new capabilities that you're going to have to roll out, learn, and work out if they fit with your business. Whatever you currently use Microsoft's tools for, an AI copilot will be there to help you, giving you that capability to get a boost of assistance with whatever your flow of work is, not having to fundamentally rethink how or where you do things in order to gain the benefits of this new technology. You set the course, and it helps you fly; it's your copilot!

How can the AI copilot concept boost productivity?

I remember back in the 1990s you could buy packaged voice recognition software like Dragon NaturallySpeaking in stores bundled with a boom microphone headset before anyone needed a headset connected to their PC for anything else. For most situations this software didn't seem to work particularly well, but for some very tenacious users it became something that was not only usable, but significantly sped up their day.

For me, I never had the patience to get any good at using it, but it was an interesting and memorable early foray into the possibilities of AI. At its core this product was a pattern matching system, so it was the great-great-great-uncle of some of the AI technologies we are starting to use today.

For as long as we've been using computers in business, the desire to develop tools to make that computer use easier, and to be able to deliver professional results without having expert-level knowledge of the computer or its software, has been present for many users. The promise of the PC has been to make work easier, but for many it has just made work different, and for many of those who started their careers before the ubiquity of PCs and the Internet, very much more technically challenging.

The excitement around AI is the promise to make the computer what it was always designed to be, a tool to alleviate many of the mundane features of work and to unlock human potential while abstracting the need for anyone to be a technical expert in the device or software doing the work. For the artist, the writer, the designer, even the radiologist, you focus on where you add greatest value, and the computer does the rest.

Speaking of radiologists, whatever happened to Dragon NaturallySpeaking? Nothing, its latest version was released in 2023. It just found riches in the niches; instead of being a little flawed in being a product that everyone would find useful, it focused on where it could make a difference. Home users can still buy it, but you're more likely to find it in legal firms or medical practices, as by specializing in narrowly bounded use cases it can deliver a better understanding of context and therefore more accurate results. And, by the way, Dragon Systems, the maker of the software, was purchased by Lernout & Hauspie in 2000. After that company's bankruptcy, it was acquired by ScanSoft. In 2005, ScanSoft also acquired Nuance Communications, and the company was rebranded Nuance. By 2013, Nuance was providing natural language processing technology to Apple that was being used in the Siri voice assistant. And in 2021, Nuance was bought by Microsoft for $19.7 billion, and became one of the foundations of its AI products. So, you really can chart a direct line between watching people wearing headsets shouting slowly worded sentences at Microsoft Word in 1998 and the announcement of Microsoft 365 Copilot 25 years later.

Of the Copilot tools Microsoft will be producing, Microsoft 365 Copilot is the one that probably has the most relevance to the work average information-focused office workers do every day. Interestingly, as it stands, taking dictation is one of the few capabilities that haven't been integrated into it (or at least yet announced). It touches every corner of your Microsoft 365 apps and focuses on key capabilities where the unique features of the AI to process large quantities of data more quickly and reliably than a human ever could allow it to be a perfect assistant.

Summarization: Do you get more emails every day than you can cope with? Are you overwhelmed with how much information you are exposed to in meetings? Microsoft 365 Copilot has your back with this. You can summarize long email threads, and you can even get a breakdown of the content of meetings – even the ones you didn't attend.

Writing Assistance: Do you struggle to type out email responses while on the go? Are you lacking the time to synthesize lots of different notes into a client proposal? Microsoft 365 Copilot can help you out by using the content you already can access to prepare drafts of emails and documents.

Data Analysis: Are you overwhelmed with Excel spreadsheets? Microsoft 365 Copilot can help you by providing analysis of your data. It can also bring together analysis across data sources, so even if your question crosses the boundaries of several files, it has the capability to help you out.

Visual Design: Whether you are trying to make sure your latest proposal is branded consistently with similar documents, or build a PowerPoint presentation with graphics and transitions, Microsoft 365 Copilot can be your go-to assistant.

Surfacing Information: By being deeply connected with the data in Microsoft 365 and across your ecosystem of business applications, Microsoft 365 can allow you to surface information that might have been tricky to access previously just using search.

Alongside this core feature set accessible from within your normal apps, through adding similar functionality to Power Platform, Microsoft will have opened the doors for more business users to intelligently automate their processes too. By combining these AI capabilities with process automation, all built by using natural language, you have a revolutionary toolset to supercharge your productivity and maximize what your company can achieve.

Example Scenario

Background

Sarah works in the marketing department of a boutique jewelry business. She is responsible both for correspondence with customers and with vendors related to marketing materials, she also manages a range of social media accounts, and associated information. Her business uses Microsoft 365, and she has a Microsoft 365 Business Standard license.

Challenge

Sarah has difficulty finding work-life balance due to the weight of communications she deals with. She struggles to respond promptly to the highest priority issues, which can include customer requests, and finds it difficult to focus on pro-active planning to social media engagement.

Implementation

A Microsoft 365 Copilot license is deployed to Sarah. Because the tools are part of Microsoft 365, with little training she can start using AI to assist her in her work. Copilot can prioritize Sarah's inbox, so she focuses on the highest priority issues, and it helps her to answer questions from customers using documents and data she already has access to in Microsoft 365

Results

Sarah can spend less time on managing her communications, while providing better and more responsive service to her stakeholders. She is less stressed about her inbox and has more time to focus on pro-active planning to improve social media. She delivers more while feeling like she has a better work-life balance.

If you're a Google Workspace user, there will be similar capabilities available to leverage AI in your everyday tasks, this will be called Duet AI for Google Workspace. Not to mention the proliferation of singular AI features in many common focused task apps.

Defining the Copilot

We have established the different varieties of AI that exist, but how do these fit into the general AI copilot model, and, specifically to the AI tools users of Microsoft Word or Google Sheets will gain access to through these technologies?

The copilot (small c) approach defined by Microsoft and branded as "Duet" by Google to convey the same purpose concerns AI features that supplement and enhance the existing work done by humans. They are tools humans will deploy, either as requested or automatically, that elevate existing work and speed up or improve the quality of aspects of the work that are best suited to a generative AI use case.

Microsoft's Copilot (big C) products (and Google's Duet AI products) extend beyond personal productivity software into other areas where the unique capabilities of AI enhance existing human work. For example, Microsoft recently presented a Cost Management Copilot for its Azure cloud computing platform, designed to analyze the complexities of the products you use in Azure, and make recommendations to help you use your resources more efficiently. This is not a core productivity task, but it would be a complex and laborious task for a human to undertake, whereas AI can chew through the mountains of connected data in seconds.

We have three core tiers of Microsoft Copilot that will impact most users. Copilot that lives inside a Windows PC and helps you to operate your computer. Copilot that lives in your web browser and is your companion on the web, and Copilot that lives in your business apps and helps you get more done on work tasks you'd be doing every day. Though Google's approach is not so clearly defined, it does have the potential to elevate products in each of these broad categories too.

This image from Microsoft shows how it breaks down the usage potential of these three tiers of products, across its Copilot in Windows, Bing Chat Enterprise, and Microsoft 365 Copilot products.

Microsoft Copilot commercial SKU line-up

	Copilot in Windows	Bing Chat Enterprise	Microsoft 365 Copilot
Microsoft Copilot UX	✓	✓	✓
Bing Chat (LLM + Web)	✓	✓	✓
Commercial Data Protection		✓	✓
Microsoft 365 Enterprise Security, Privacy, and Compliance			✓
Microsoft 365 Chat			✓
Microsoft 365 Apps			✓

Figure 2: Microsoft Copilot commercial SKU line-up announced September 2023, and as shown on Microsoft's announcement blog 9/29/2023.

The common thread of these Copilot branded products is that they are built upon a shared foundation that is OpenAI's generative foundation model GPT-4, but each layer has different capabilities depending on the usage scenario, and the license fees needed to gain access to it.

If you work for Dudley and Dudley Lawncare Limited (an imaginary company we can use to highlight these examples), each of these tools would be able to deal with your request of "Tell me about our standard operating procedure related to lawncare work".

Copilot in Windows will generate a generic response based on a search of the web using the Bing search engine, and your request and response will not be protected by Microsoft under its commercial data protection (i.e. that content could be used by Microsoft for other purposes). This kind of scenario will mainly relate to consumer use of Windows or business use with very low tiers of Microsoft 365 licensing like Business Basic.

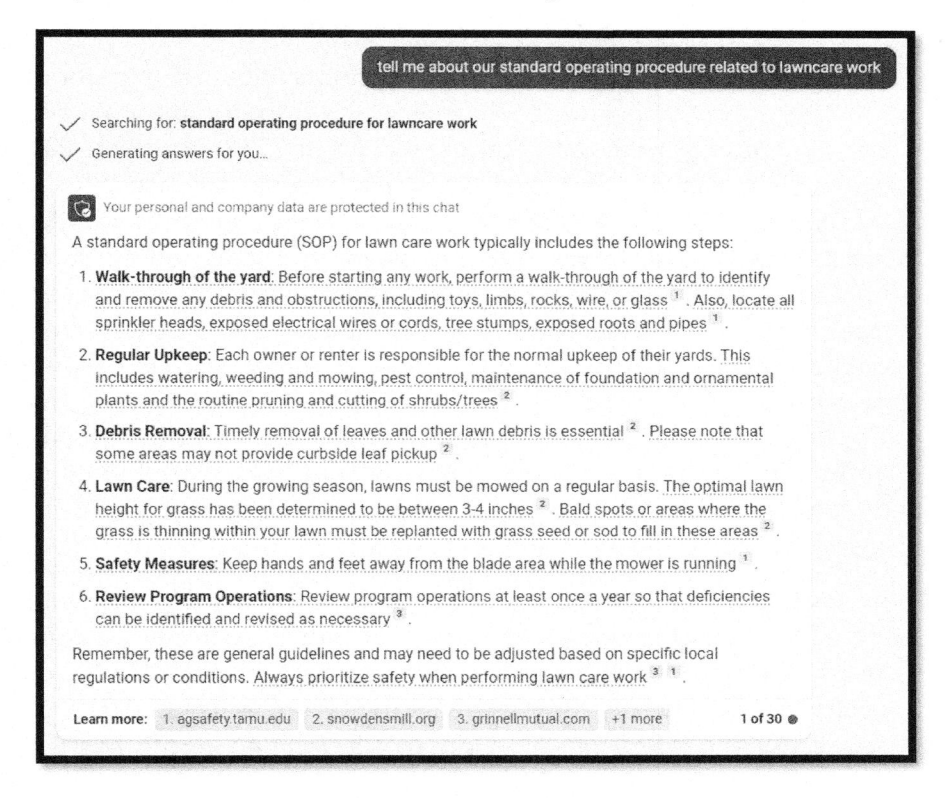

Figure 3: Lawncare request made through Bing Chat Enterprise.

The same request made to Bing Chat Enterprise will get the same quality of response – a generic one based on a web search – but Microsoft guarantees the protection of your prompt and the response you get back. So, for example, if you wanted to share the proprietary Dudley and Dudley lawncare approach with Copilot, you could do that with Bing Chat Enterprise, but shouldn't do that just with Copilot in Windows (unless signed in with an enterprise licensed business account). This kind of scenario applies to most Microsoft 365 licenses that do not have additional Microsoft 365 Copilot add-on licensing.

To add an extra layer of confusion, if Bing Chat Enterprise is enabled for your account, then the Copilot in Windows interface will protect your data and show it as operating under Bing Chat Enterprise. This is a potentially confusing distinction that will likely be cleared up by Microsoft in due course.

When using Microsoft 365 Copilot, your chat options expand to not only rely on knowledge searched out through the web, but from searching your own company data. In this case, you can directly access Dudley and Dudley's custom lawncare SOP (Standard Operating Procedures), if your user has access to that file in OneDrive or SharePoint. You might then add content from it to an email in Outlook or send a team member information related to it in Teams, you might even be creating a marketing document and be able to use it as content to inspire a flyer created in Word. All these options can be drafted directly by Copilot in response to a natural language prompt, but will generally be worked upon in the specific app you would use to do that type of work.

All these tools are useful and open the door to amazing possibilities, but because of its grounding (that's the technical term for getting contextual information) in your company's data, and because of its inclusion inside the apps you are probably using every day, the tier we will focus on here in terms of capabilities is Microsoft 365 Copilot (for which Google has the equivalent Duet AI for Workspace product that has similar capabilities but on top of your Google hosted business data and apps).

Beyond Copilots

It's important to highlight that even with the amazing capabilities the various Copilot tools across Microsoft's product stack will bring, they will not solve every challenge, nor do they intend to.

Throughout this book, most examples focus on types of work that fit with the copilot model that augments the capability of existing tools. These, most often, fit the usage needs you are most likely to see from office-based information workers, the people who are commonly spending their days in front of Teams or Excel, or another component of Microsoft Office.

However, later we will explore how AI can be implemented outside the office or information work context, and how its included in tools like Microsoft Dynamics 365 ERP (Enterprise Resource Planning) or its competitors. There are specific tooling options for roles like sales or customer service, who may also use Microsoft 365 Copilot, or more specialized capabilities for needs like field service management.

Beyond this, in scenarios where businesses have required custom developed pro-code tools in the past, there are still opportunities with AI. As previously mentioned, AI services are available in Azure or other platforms like AWS, and there are even AI models small enough to download and run locally. Where businesses want to build new tools based on AI technology, options are available from low-code to pro-code.

Microsoft's Copilots and similar copilot style tools from other vendors will open amazing possibilities, but it's important to realize that they will not be a solution to every problem, and just as in the past bigger or more unique challenges have often required bigger or more unique tools, the same will remain true in the AI age.

Adapting to a Copilot in Your Team

Like any new technology, an AI copilot or assistant will require some adaptation, rethinking, and may impact different teams in very different ways.

The common strand in all these tools is that there is still a big human component. The AI must be able to understand what the human wants to do the right job, and it will take time and effort for team members to learn how best to interact with their AI companion.

Communication is the key to success, both in terms of how we communicate with our teams, but also how they adopt communicating with the AI tools that are deployed for them to use. We must be proactive and considerate in both these respects, to ensure the focus is on learning and collaborating, rather than being fearful of the negative impacts AI might have.

We are generally used to learning how to use tools by adopting a series of common steps. Two people learning how to use a table saw will approach it in a similar way, as there is a narrow range of acceptable and safe practices when using such a tool. Generative AI is different, as we must convey what we are thinking to the tool for it to do its work; there's not a series of button presses to learn, but there is a new way of communicating our intent, and different ways of prompting the AI will elicit different types and qualities of response, and work differently in different apps.

As the AI joins us to take its place in the copilot's chair, as the pilot you must plan for what that arrival looks like, how it will be announced, and what the strategic and operational implications of this change will be. Throughout the subsequent chapters, we will plan out that journey and consider where it may have an impact so you can feel confident approaching the runway.

Action Steps

- Consider to what degree copilot-like features will be of benefit to the business or team you are responsible for. It's important to set realistic initial expectations, and if you're leading a marketing team, a copilot may be a great fit, but if you're supervising a team of car mechanics, your AI needs may be somewhat different.

- If you haven't already, consider gaining some experience with Bing Chat, ChatGPT or Google Bard so you have a baseline of knowledge of the types of requests these generalized generative AI tools can service.

4. Strategic Considerations for AI in Business

In a platform like Microsoft 365, there will be tools you use every day, and many that you've either decided not to deploy or that you simply don't know about. Look at the toolbar in Word or Excel; how many of those buttons do you genuinely use regularly? How many businesses ignored a tool like Microsoft Teams completely before March 2020 when we all started using it because of the pandemic? In the first year of Covid, usage jumped significantly, and continued to grow.

Some users explore software on their own and will try out new features, but they are generally in the minority. No matter how many possibilities you see from a new technology, unless you decide to actively roll out adoption of those tools, they will not have the impact you desire. Adoption is about having an excited and passionate leader who sees the possibilities new tools may bring for a brighter future, but it's also about many other factors, and no single person's or small group's excitement and passion can supplant their importance.

The adoption of tools like Teams or Zoom brought with it wider considerations beyond technology. Issues such as camera etiquette, availability for out-of-hours messages, and the effectiveness of remote engagement compared to in-office interactions, suddenly became topics of debate. The integration of AI into your business will have the same or greater breadth of impact. Consequently, the first step to bringing AI into your business should be establishing an understanding of what you are aiming to achieve on a broader level.

Don't Follow the Pandemic Model

For many businesses the experience of rolling out products like Teams or Zoom during the pandemic may well be their last significant technology change. However, in nearly all cases, this was not something that was done in a well-planned or proactive way as it was responding to global events happening at the time.

Considering AI right now may seem reactive, but it is not. It is seizing an opportunity that has presented itself, but doing this successfully must include the need to plan proactively and strategically. There is time to get it right from the start while also allowing flexibility to explore the opportunity fully.

Understanding Your Business Needs

Every business has unique qualities in how it approaches what it does. Even businesses in the same industry, with largely comparable products, and operating at the same scale, will often be vastly different in how they approach tasks and how their company culture operates. Just as there is no one-size-fits-all answer for most issues in business, planning for AI will be unique to your specific needs.

Gaining an understanding of that current situation through a needs assessment is vital to mapping out the right journey.

Depending on your scale, this might involve a formal or informal process, and could be something you initially conduct yourself, with internal resources, or even with external help like a specialist consultant.

You might consider the following questions as you think about your needs:

- Where are there bottlenecks in what you do?
- What processes or work areas are efficiency drains on the rest of the business?

- Where are there problems with accuracy or quality?
- What repetitive or mundane tasks consume the most time?
- How technically savvy are your team members?
- How well does your team respond to change?
- What unique differentiators are hallmarks of your success?
- Are there recurrent process or efficiency issues connected to team turnover or morale?

The more you can do to understand the picture of what you need and where the pitfalls are hidden, the better prepared you can be to deal with the positives and negatives that will arise on your AI journey.

Example Scenario

Background

John runs the customer service department of an online retail business. He has a team of customer service representatives who field customer inquiries coming from a diverse set of channels. These communications are a big bottleneck as while being personable it is vital for consistent messaging to be sent to customers, which means constantly referring to templates and policies related to the issues coming up.

Implementation

Using Microsoft 365 Copilot in Outlook, John's team can use generative AI to reference its templates and policy documents quickly to draft unique, personable, but policy-grounded responses to a variety of issues. Additionally, using Copilot's extensibility, his team can quickly draft and send responses across several other channels connected to their existing web-based customer communication platform.

Proactive Planning > Kneejerk Reacting

The fact that you're reading this book suggests you are at least interested in rolling out new AI tools in your business. That's great, because it means you're reading this book, but it also means you are not an impartial party in the question of whether your business should be focusing on AI right now.

If it ain't broke, don't fix it!

This expression easily sums up the negative counterpoint on moving forward with a lot of AI-based change right now. While there are good reasons to consider bringing AI capabilities to any business, badly designed change is often worse than no change at all.

AI is far from the answer to every problem, and having a reasonable view of what current AI technology can achieve is incredibly important. You also need to focus on the right type of tool as, as we have learned, while a product like Microsoft 365 Copilot has amazing capabilities, they are capabilities best suited to a specific set of problems grouped around work most commonly done by information workers. Overestimating the benefits of AI might be as dangerous to your long-term success as ignoring its potential or seeing it through the negative sci-fi colored lens.

Example Scenario

Background

Rishi owns a product licensing company with a wide range of products based on others' IP. He has a small but trusted team who have been successful in securing great licensing and creating products that have delighted customers. However, one of his most trusted team members has recently resigned due to other things going on in her life and Rishi is interested in using AI to replace her in her responsibilities, including product design and quality control. She is leaving in just six weeks.

Challenge

The goals of this project are not realistic either with the timeline or the current capabilities of AI. While it's possible to take the work product of an individual and use it to help train a customized AI system or to ground a broader AI system like Microsoft 365 Copilot, the component parts of a person's emails, documents, and chats, are not enough to convert their knowledge and experience in all respects to an AI tool.

Rishi may select parts of this role that could benefit from AI-focused digital transformation, but in the short timeframe he has available he will likely gain much more benefit from more traditional approaches, such as ensuring other team members are trained on core parts of their role, and, if not done already, creating a comprehensive "manual" for those vital processes that are at risk.

AI may be part of the solution to this sort of challenge, but it is not a panacea and will not meet Rishi's need totally.

It makes most sense to align your plans for AI alongside your existing strategic priorities, particularly if these plans are what you use to communicate internally, either at executive level or across your entire business. This then roots your journey in established thinking rather than creating the appearance of hopping on the latest popular band wagon.

For example, consider a business where one of your strategic priorities is to reduce team turnover to address challenges you have had in hiring the right talent. You can easily couple your priorities in AI to this by focusing on the capabilities an AI copilot will give you to improve the work life of team members by giving them support in mundane, low value tasks.

Or, in another business, you might be focused on providing a more consistent customer experience across your locations. You would then highlight the role AI can take in providing consistency of the information you include in new proposals and in applying your brand templates.

Unless you are a technology company, it will be far more palatable to all involved to contextualize the benefits and possibilities of AI against well established, widely communicated, and universally supported top-level goals rather than just telling everyone to start using AI. This kind of decree might work at Microsoft, but it's unlikely to work at Dudley & Dudley Lawncare Limited.

Choosing the Right Tools

With any technological change, ensuring you have the right tooling is critical. In this context of adopting a broadly functional AI copilot system that helps across your business, your options are limited, but for most companies (those who use Microsoft 365 or Google Workspace) such tooling will become part of your productivity suite, either by default or as an add-on option.

It will probably take some years to determine whether the AI components of these tools alter their efficacy enough to make the AI itself a differentiator that might make you choose one productivity platform over the other. For now, I would suggest that if you're comfortable using one of these platforms – for example Microsoft 365 – the complexity and risk involved in moving to the other is unlikely to be paid back by the benefits of the AI technology in the short term.

Outside of these two major productivity platforms that most businesses use, there are also a growing number of smaller single-focus apps that are beginning to employ similar AI technologies. However, while many of these new tools are generative systems (e.g., a "generate text" capability has now surfaced on the website builder Squarespace), they are more like the earlier incarnations of AI technology such as the expenses system with a receipt scanner than tools like Microsoft 365 Copilot. Why? The most significant difference is context. No matter how good the text generator on a tool like Squarespace is, without the context that comes from being able to see and reference your data, it will be limited to working within the parameters you give it for each individual prompt or chat.

That is not to say that singular AI capabilities within focused tools are not useful, there are certainly a lot of use cases where they are. However, the growth of an "AI" or "generate" button in every app does not mean that by pasting together a patchwork of separate apps with AI capabilities you would reach a tipping point where their combined capabilities are equivalent to or better than a more general productivity suite-based AI tool. The benefit (and, if you keep reading, detriment) that Microsoft and Google have as the incumbent kings of productivity software is that they have access to mountains of your data and can use that to bring context to the capabilities of their AI tools in a way that is currently unmatched elsewhere.

From a 30,000-foot view it's important that we can group the AI tools we have access to into four main categories. We have our productivity copilots, like Microsoft 365 Copilot or Duet AI for Google Workspace. We have app-based generative experiences, like the "generate text" button in Squarespace. We have our non-generative expert systems type of AI, like your receipt processor in QuickBooks. And lastly, we have those AI tools that are partially or fully customized to your needs using a mixture of AI foundations and either low-code or pro-code techniques.

The productivity copilot class of solution is heavily skewed toward the needs of predominantly office-based information workers, and focuses on a large group of tasks that are similarly shared between many businesses, processing email, writing documents preparing sales presentations etc. This is where we will focus most of our attention over the coming chapters, but in later chapters we will also consider the other broad classes of capabilities highlighted above. If we think of the 80/20 rule that dictates that 80% of the benefit will be derived from 20% of the effort; these tools are the ones where in many businesses we can deliver great AI-enabled benefit with much reduced effort proportionally versus more complex and customized systems.

A big benefit of focusing on our productivity copilots is that they are plug-and-play capabilities connected to whichever set of tools you currently use and allow you to focus predominantly on the business impact of AI without giving too much attention to the technological aspects underlying how those AI capabilities work. They can supply a foundation on which you not only build new capacity using AI, but effective management of issues like AI ethics, data integration, and team communications that we will further delve into throughout this book.

In most cases starting here and then enhancing with more specialist capabilities where you need them will be a sensible approach. Ultimately though, like any business change, this decision is down to what you are aiming to achieve in the context of your use case, and what types of work and workers you are focused on re-imagining with AI.

While there is no one right way of approaching AI for your business, caution is advised if you decide to focus instead on the class of AI which is those app-based generative experiences. We have already highlighted that a patchwork of these types of tools probably won't be able to achieve a broad Microsoft 365 Copilot type of useability, but it may still be alluring to gain AI capabilities in a range of more specialist apps. However, at the current time (mid-2023) it's unclear how many of these have been added because they deliver long-term benefit to the product rather than just allowing marketing teams to claim their products are AI-enabled. Whenever you select a new tool, it's important to do your due diligence, which includes considering the value of a long-term operating record for anyone you hand your business data over to.

Regardless of the direction you choose, it should be the outcome of a process of discovery where you have assessed your needs (more on this in chapter 6) and aligned them with the capabilities of specific tools you then seek to roll out and adopt in your business. The intentionality of this process is important to getting everyone on the same plane so your copilots can help you bring benefit to your entire business and its whole team.

Preparing Your Team

With any process of change, the greatest impact will come not from the changes you make to what's on peoples' screens, but the changes you make to the thinking of the people in the chairs in front of those screens.

When it comes to AI you need to be aware of all the normal ways a technology change may impact your team members, but also a specific set of concerns that are unique to the role AI may take in the future. There may be team members who are resistant to this technology as they see the potential for it to replace rather than augment their work, and in some cases, the clearer you can be in conveying the specific business needs where AI will have benefit, the greater this concern may be.

As we have described, connecting your plans for AI to existing people-centered priorities can be effective and can dull the edge of concerns your team may have about the potential downsides of AI technology. However, while this can be the headline for your communication plan, there must be more detail, an opportunity for team members to give feedback, and time to turn operational or technical concerns into effective guidance, or even changes of direction.

Involving team members in your first exploration of your business needs can be a powerful way to build a network of champions throughout your organization. The more your team has ownership in the route you have planned out, the more comfortable they may be as you bring on board your copilot and start rolling out the resultant AI-based changes.

Evaluating AI Performance

It is important, from the very start, to think about how you will evaluate the impact of AI tool adoption. Like any change you make there will be resultant upsides and downsides, and it's vital to ensure that they are in the right balance and guide them appropriately through remedial actions if they are not.

Your approach to this evaluation should be sufficiently broad to understand the organizational impact you're seeing. For example, you may have implemented AI tools that have helped alleviate operational bottlenecks, and you may see this in your revenue staying flat while your overtime costs decrease. But how far does this benefit go? If you also see your offices empty on Fridays or after 4pm, then perhaps there is capacity being left on the table that could leverage growth. The answer to how to address this won't be the same for every business, but the most reasonable way to look at this is that ideally AI technology will generate benefits that can be shared between the business and its team members in a way that is broadly enhancing to both.

Align Input and Output Metrics

Your measure of improvements must be in alignment with your approach to measuring problems or opportunities.

If the problem you are trying to address with AI was originally understood qualitatively – "I don't feel engaged at work because I spend too long on repetitive tasks" – then either you need to measure this issue quantitively ahead of any change – how much time is spent on repetitive tasks – or look for a qualitative fix measure after implementation.

Following metrics because your technology makes them easier to capture cannot prove you have addressed an issue that had no metrics to begin with, at least not in the short term.

Address your solutions in the same language as the problems they are solving.

Any change requires ongoing review to ensure you achieve, and continue to achieve, your desired outcomes. Technology changes often have far reaching impacts, and with AI this possibility of a broader range of impacts is amplified. Ensure that a diversity of voices is heard in forums that are open to hearing about unexpected, unintended, or unforeseen impacts that are being felt because of, or connected to, your investments in AI technology.

Future-Proofing Your Business

The title of this section is misleading as it's impossible to truly future proof your business. From the release of ChatGPT by OpenAI in November 2022 until now, the pace of change around AI technology has been truly dizzying. And while clearly much of the technology involved in rolling out products like Microsoft 365 Copilot has been in the works for a long while, it is also clear that even the biggest technology companies were caught somewhat off guard by the pace of innovation and the amount of interest OpenAI's initial offering garnered.

AI will continue to be a rapidly evolving field, but before it so has Internet technology, and before that, so was the rise of computing in the workplace. It is also a technology that, for most of the applications we are now discussing, is in its infancy, much like a mid-1990s Internet versus the web 2.0/3.0 of today.

Microsoft has consistently been releasing Office software since 1990, and Microsoft (or Office) 365 has a lineage dating back more than a decade. These are not start-up apps that may be here today and gone tomorrow, and Microsoft has invested a great amount of effort in integrating its Copilot line of AI tools throughout the capabilities of its office suite. The same goes for Google, which is now 25-years old, and with not quite the same lineage for Workspace as Microsoft Office, still, is clearly, in productivity for the long haul.

These tools will undoubtedly change over time, but it seems certain that the future will include the leveraging of AI technology within and throughout the productivity software we use every day. A decision to start exploring this technology today is an investment in future proofing for tomorrow.

Another focus of future proofing should be the investments you make now not just in technology, but in the human-focused aspects of adopting that technology. The focus of AI technology is to augment and not replace our human workers, but the more familiarity our workers have with AI tools and how to use them, the more efficacy our AI technology investments will bring to our businesses. Ensuring team members have access to technical skills related to AI is important, but also developing an understanding of non-technical skills such as AI ethics (we focus on this in chapters 7-8) may be just as vital.

In the next chapter, we'll discuss the role of leadership in guiding your team through the adoption of AI. For now, it's vital that effective planning is undertaken, but there is no rush. It is better to spend a little more time on the runway to assure a smoother flight toward your AI future.

Action Steps

- Create your own list of the issues you want to explore that are connected to your desire to implement AI-based solutions in your business.

- Consider the strategic goals of your business (these may be explicit or implicit). Where can you connect the AI focused solutions you listed above with each of these?

- Sense-check your own AI-focused aspirations. Are they grounded in the reality of the technology as it stands today, or in fictional depictions of what AI could achieve in the future?

5. Leadership in the Age of AI: Guiding Your Team Forward

The role of leadership is of extreme importance as AI gets woven into the fabric of our day-to-day business operations. AI will enable changes not just to how work is done, but to habits around work, procedures of work, and the culture throughout your teams. Your role as a leader is to be effective in guiding these changes, ensuring your team members are well-prepared and confident in the face of new capabilities and ways doing the business of work.

Throughout the last few years, we have seen the broad scope of impact that technological changes can have across work and life. Before March 2020, few would have imagined a world where so many of us instantly switched on a work-from-home modality, either from a purely technical basis, nor in connection to the sweeping range of other places this affected our lives. This impactful change in where and how many of us worked brought about a reset in many facets of life that extended beyond the technological effects and into areas like how society viewed work, how workers felt empowered and valued, what responsibilities employers have, and what rights and privileges employees enjoy. It is important to recognize that this is the context from which we begin our discussion about the implementation of AI technologies, and it is likely that in the long term, the weight and range of resultant changes across work and life will be even greater!

Workable AI is certainly a monumental technical challenge, but when thinking about generalized AI tools like Microsoft 365

Copilot, the technical aspects are not where we should expend most of our thought. These productivity copilots will be largely plug and play from a technical perspective, so the broader context of managing the changes that AI adoption will initiate should be where we focus most of our attention initially.

It is entirely possible, even if you have done no work to institute AI technology in your business, that you've already experienced the work product of these technologies. Perhaps a team member leaned on ChatGPT for an assignment? Perhaps a marketing company you use generated AI content on your behalf without your knowledge? Understanding and communicating your expectations around how AI will be used within and for your business, and connected issues like how you will make sure it's used responsibly and ethically, are all entirely non-technical challenges connected to these technologically complex new capabilities.

Like any change, as a leader, you need to get in front of the challenges you could reasonably expect to experience. The human dimension of these changes, the degree to which team members will be unsettled or upset, comes down to the existing culture of your organization and how you plan for and navigate this set of changes. You need to consider that it's likely that even initial steps into the deployment of AI technologies may trigger concerns amongst team members that your end goal is to replace them with technology. As a leader you must navigate a plan that both effectively deploys your selected technologies and addresses these very understandable and human concerns.

Is AI ready to replace people?

Every day there is new media coverage or online content popping up that focuses attention on what are perceived as negative consequences of AI adoption. While there are a lot of outlandish imaginary scenarios, one that is easy for many to connect with is the potential for human workers to be replaced by AI tools.

In a broad sense, this idea is in no way aligned with the experience of developing new technologies throughout human history. We have tools today that allow many of the tasks most humans focused their lives on a century or two ago to be done mainly by machines and with incredibly enhanced efficiency. Yet, ignoring cyclical peaks and valleys, employment and labor participation in modern economies has remained strong, and much of the world is wealthier today than it ever has been.

There will be jobs where the impact of AI does drive a reduction in the amount of work that needs to be done by humans, and in some industries, this may happen quicker than in others depending on the specific needs of the work the AI tools help with. But new jobs will arrive, some connected with the management of these AI tools, and others in areas we haven't yet imagined that result from the increase in innovation AI will help us drive.

We cannot entirely dismiss the concern your team members may have about the jobs they do. But we can help to contextualize these changes through an awareness of history and our roadmap to a better future.

Your focus should be to deliver leadership that promotes the following considerations:

Transparency: You need to communicate in a way that is transparent across a range of issues. Firstly, there's the capabilities of the technology itself – what is its purpose in the specific needs of your business and what benefits do you see it bringing? Secondly, there's the impact it might have on your team members – it may well enhance your ability to deliver certain people-centric goals, but there may also be cases where it truly does add leverage in such a way to reduce your reliance on human work. Lastly, there should be an aspect of transparency in the exploration – we don't currently know all the answers, you are at the start of an exciting journey where we don't fully know the destination, and that should impact how you communicate about this versus other changes where the long-term is more well known.

Opportunity: Your AI journey will change your business, and along the way there will be great opportunities. While AI will alleviate mundane aspects of work and allow many workers who spend at least some of their time on administrative busywork to add more value, this will not happen without taking the opportunity to upskill. Like any tool, you start as a novice, and it takes learning and experience to become an expert. For some, there will be the opportunity for entirely new types of roles, like, for example, thinking about how to ensure your business uses AI in an ethical way. For others, the opportunity will just be to enhance their skills in using AI tools to supercharge the types of work they have always done.

Inclusiveness: Giving a wide range of your team members a seat at the table is good practice during any type of change process, you gain insights and value that help your project succeed, while sowing the seeds for people to become champions for your causes across your organization. The journey with AI adoption should be no different, but you may want to consider your stakeholder group even more broadly. Will those who are touched by content generated in part with AI be trusting of it? Will team members be more reluctant to engage with communications if they think "Not another AI generated email"? Might they be suspicious of data analysis conducted with the help of AI tools? And, equally, you may have team members who rarely touch a computer who are genuinely excited and intrigued by the possibilities of AI.

With these focus areas, you can help to assure maximum buy-in on your change journey to help deliver the smoothest possible transition. This involves clear, consistent, and open communication about the changes AI will introduce, including how AI tools will be integrated into daily tasks, what training will be provided, and how the transition will be managed. Different team members will adapt to AI at different speeds. Being patient and flexible, supplying additional support where needed, and celebrating small victories along the way can make a significant difference.

Where possible, the benefits delivered by AI should be shared between the business and its team members. AI offers the opportunity to rethink work, but if that rethinking is just focused on the benefit provided to the business, without consideration of the potential upsides for your team, it may be hard to get engagement where a logical long-term concern is that at least some human work might be supplanted by technology. Encouraging a diversity of voices to be heard in evaluating AI's impact ensures a comprehensive view of its effects, both positive and negative, across the organization, and allows you to respond proactively and positively.

In conclusion, a future-focused leader should be able to guide the team through the AI transformation journey, manage change effectively, and ensure everyone's on board, addressing human concerns, and measuring success appropriately. By doing so, you can help build a culture ready to embrace the possibilities that AI offers, ensuring a smooth and successful flight into the age of AI, which is good both for your business and for your team members.

Action Steps

- Map out the most recent experience of big technology focused change you had in your organization – this may be the adoption of work-from-home technology in 2020 or something later. Consider what aspects of its impacts were solely connected with technology and where the impacts crept into other aspects of work life.

- For the three focus areas of **Transparency, Opportunity,** and **Inclusiveness**. Where did you achieve strongly and where could you have improved with the technological change you are reflecting on?

- Look back at the lists you made in the Action Steps in the last chapter. How could you connect opportunities for **Transparency, Opportunity**, and **Inclusiveness** in each of these?

6. Planning Tools and Approaches: Understanding and analyzing your processes

By this point you have developed an understanding of what, at a high level, you are aiming to achieve. You also have become familiar, in general terms, with what AI is and what it can do. You have also considered how you might go about leading an AI-focused change process to maximize its positive impacts while minimizing the undesirable outputs, particularly for your team members. But this leaves a glaring hole – what technology are you going to deploy and where?

A tool like Microsoft 365 Copilot has a general set of capabilities that address needs that most information workers will have in one way or another. If you write or receive emails, Copilot has tools to help you. If you write documents or create presentations, Copilot has tools to help you. But, if you spend your day using a custom order management system that was developed by a small independent software vendor for your business in 2007, you're out of luck with Copilot, right?

Not necessarily. The power of a tool like Microsoft 365 Copilot comes from access to your data, and by default it has access to the data you (as a user) have access to in Microsoft 365. The technology underpinning this is called the Microsoft Graph, and this is a huge index with pointers to the various documents, emails, chats, or presentations you can see as a Microsoft 365 user. And, Microsoft knows that most businesses, even the most ardent Microsoft buyers, will have software that isn't part of Microsoft 365 or its connected Power Platform, Fabric, or

Dynamics 365 cousins, so it has built Graph to be able to "talk to" other systems.

If you use a platform like Google Workspace, then a similar set of concepts exist around the fact that inside your Google account exists your emails, your calendars, your contacts, and even your files. To this point, Microsoft exposes many of these capabilities in a richer set of platform capabilities, but the foundation of having access to a broad set of data is there. This is what is likely to set these productivity suite-connected AI tools apart from others that are attached to software with more singularly focused capabilities, and, thus, access to less data.

Technology called Microsoft Graph Connectors enables system admins to either choose from a list of available connections or to create their own connections into third-party products. There are two caveats though, the third-party product needs some kind of modern API (application programming interface) which allows the two systems to talk a common language about data, and these tools are pretty enterprise focused and therefore expensive to run. Google has a similar capability called Google Cloud Search which can be extended into third-party data repositories such as Salesforce.

More accessible to smaller businesses is another technology to enable outside data to be used by Microsoft 365 Copilot. These plugins or message extensions still require API access but can be connected without the cost of Graph Connectors. They are also quite simple to build, although beyond the capabilities of novices and requiring some pro-code knowledge.

Understanding a productivity copilot's secret sauce: Its access to your data

The technical aspects of how your data helps a productivity copilot like Microsoft 365 Copilot deserve some special consideration. This section may not be of interest to all readers, so if not, just move on and come back to it later if it piques your interest.

We have considered in earlier chapters what makes up an AI system and what generative AI is. We have also touched on large language models and how GPT-4 is the model that underpins both ChatGPT and Microsoft's copilot products. But that can lead to obvious questions around how these models generate information based on your data in the background.

A large language model is trained to predict how words connect to one another. This training consists of a process of consuming enormous quantities of written data and over time gaining a better understanding of how words go together. When a model is in early training, if you ask it to tell you the capital of the United States, it might give you the answer "green", it has no idea what a capital or the United States is. Later on in the training it might give the answer "Los Angeles", it now understands that a capital is a city, and that Los Angeles is a city, but it does not know enough to get the right answer. But, if you go ask Bing Chat the same question, it will immediately respond "Washington D.C.". This ability to answer correctly is essentially just connected to consuming enough writing where the words of your prompt and the words of the response combine frequently enough to make it probable that it knows the answer.

This may seem like a wild leap, but we see it all the time. If you have a pet dog, what combination of factors allowed it to learn that when you say "sit" it should sit down? If you're walking along the street with your dog and you're on a phone call and you say, "She asked me to sit with her today", your dog probably doesn't hear the word "sit" in that sentence and just sits down, it keeps walking. Its ability to understand isn't arbitrarily connected to the word "sit" but to a combination of factors that include specific context clues.

Often, once you've learned how large language models are trained using data, you make another wild leap about how it works in the context of a productivity copilot: You conclude that this training process must be completed using your data; your documents, your spreadsheets, your chats, in order for the AI tool to work. But this isn't the case.

A large language model could be thought of as knowing everything but understanding nothing. For us to interact with it well and get useful responses, we must provide it with context. When we ask, "What is the capital of the United States?", we are providing context that is different to just typing "Tell me something". The more complex what we want to get back, the more detailed our context must be. If you're an ice cream shop owner, you could just ask "How much ice cream will we sell next year?", without any added context you wouldn't get a good answer. But if you add the context of Excel files holding your last 3 years sales data, the answer you get will be much better.

The large language model has never seen your sales data before, so it's not giving you an answer based on being trained on that data, but it has seen lots of sales data examples within the dataset it has been trained on, so when it looks at your spreadsheet the content is familiar. This is the same as sharing your financials with an accountant, they may have never seen your particular data, but they have seen enough similar data to very quickly understand it and begin to analyze it.

When we think about a product like Microsoft 365 Copilot, there isn't a copy of the large language model in the background that is specifically trained on your data. Everyone uses the same model, and that model never keeps your data for training (in the case of Microsoft's privacy policies at least). The large language model is only part of the solution, the rest of your productivity copilot is the power of data indexing and search.

A company like Microsoft or Google keeps huge quantities of your company data on your behalf, that in many cases includes most of what you need to refer to in doing your job every day. Whereas it used to be tiresome to search through your emails, in our cloud powered era it's a simple process, and this is due to big investments in improving data indexing for search.

When you need help from your copilot, it uses this search index to find information within your business that you already have access to that will provide context to your request. For example, if you ask, "Give me a summary of my recent emails with Bob", the content of emails that include Bob will be retrieved using search, and that text will be sent along with your request to the large language model to use. Given that request and that context, it then uses its generative AI capabilities to provide you with the summary you are asking for.

It is this access to data alongside high-quality generative AI that enables this productivity copilot advance, without the data, and without those powerful search capabilities, all you've got is a dog that has no idea when to sit down.

Across your data estate the value that Microsoft 365 Copilot will offer will be based entirely on a user's access to data through the underlying Microsoft Graph, Microsoft Graph Connectors, or plugins to 3rd-party sources. Ensuring users have the right access to data, as in not too much and not too little will be a vital governance aspect of rolling out these AI tools. However, while the capabilities of Microsoft 365 Copilot may be impressive, they are not the right fit for every scenario and this is why there is a stable of other Copilots, low-code technologies to integrate AI, and third-party software solutions on the horizon. It is likely that other providers such as Google will offer similar portfolios of tools to maximize access to data and to expand functionality for its AI solutions.

The best practice with most technology projects is to build from an established foundation. In most scenarios where you want to embrace AI, products like Microsoft's Copilots can be those foundations as they can so easily integrate with existing workflows. But, for more specialized, or less office-based information-focused tasks, it is likely that a general product like Microsoft 365 Copilot will not meet your needs, either entirely or at all. In these cases, a wide variety of other options are available, but these tools will also benefit from access to the right data and resources just as is the case described above.

What needs to be leveraged is wholly dependent on what the purpose of the related work is and what barriers or bottlenecks exist before it. Simply throwing solutions at problems without understanding what those problems are and why they exist can appear extremely innovative when it comes to software and related technologies, but it is no more useful than buying a crew of carpenters 20 different hammers to help them install a box of screws.

Listen, Record, and Cover It with Sticky Notes

The key place to gain knowledge about processes is the people who are in the middle of them every day. And depending on what you're looking at or looking for, this may include your team members, your customers, or your vendors.

Simply taking opportunities to genuinely learn about how work is done rather than how you think it's done can be eye opening and should be a foundational aspect of any technology change. In chapter 4 we considered the importance of involving team members to keep them engaged with the project, but that involvement should not just be for show, those team members will often genuinely know more about how that change might impact their role or their processes than anyone else involved in the project.

How to design free-communicating forums to learn from team members or others will be different depending on your organizational culture and other factors, and is beyond the scope of this book, but you should find a set of tools that work for you and capture as much information as you can. In some organizations the right approach will be a survey, in others it'll be a sit-down meeting, in others still it will be more interactive, a whiteboard session, or themed tables with paper cloths covered in sticky notes. In most organizations it will be a mixture depending on what you're trying to learn.

You should refer back to your initial interest areas for AI and how you related them to your strategic needs in chapters 1 and 4, and focus on involving your stakeholders in both that thinking and conversation rather than constraining your exploration to just a handful of paths.

You might focus on issues such as:

- What are the processes that take the most time?
- Where are the interface points between processes...
- ...and which of these are easy or full of friction?
- What systems, software, or otherwise are used to complete the processes?
- What systems are really used to complete the processes? (Thinking of issues of shadow IT that come up in many organizations).
- How does the process deviate from the standard operating procedure?
- How does data storage, or inputs and outputs, deviate from the standard operating procedure?

These will help you map out your understanding of your processes, and to understand factors like how much does email volume impact the work of a particular group versus the useability of their proprietary CRM, and therefore how helpful might rolling out a product like Microsoft 365 Copilot be versus focusing in on something more customized and targeted. In most cases, gaining a picture of where the benefits of a productivity copilot type system will most tightly focus can give you clues on where you can test this type of system versus needing something entirely different.

If budget is no barrier, then the right answer might be to address all these diverse needs, but most businesses have to prioritize their spending, and often do not have the resources to address every need at once. A product like Microsoft 365 Copilot will add significant expenditure to your Microsoft services invoice, but this might pale in comparison to the cost associated with custom developing a solution or building the structures in the background to allow data to more easily flow between existing systems. For this reason, your productivity copilot can be a solid foundational building block even if you plan to address more specific needs in the future.

Mine Processes Intelligently

It is common for there to be gaps between how a business thinks a process is done and how it gets done in reality. There can be workarounds that creep in because of system inefficiencies. There can be misunderstandings due to poor or incomplete training. Or it might simply have evolved between the last time it was documented and now. Simple information gathering sessions can help to identify these situations, but for several reasons they won't be universally successful, and it will be necessary to use other techniques to get the right data.

In some instances, these blind spots can lead to safety or compliance issues. Take a process in a kitchen where staff take shortcuts on cold temperature storage recordkeeping. Or an office where customers phone in payments and instead of being entered into a credit card terminal immediately are written down on paper and only entered at the end of the day. Not knowing that these process changes have happened does not alleviate the liability your business might have when something goes wrong arising from those incorrect practices.

The issue of shadow IT might arise here too. Where you think you know what systems are being used for certain processes, but the reality is that certain departments or individuals have taken shortcuts that include different tools that are not officially sanctioned on an organizational level.

What is Shadow IT?

Shadow IT is not an AI specific concept but may relate to AI-enabled tools as well as traditional software. This is where individuals or sections of a business will start to use software tools that are not deployed under the control of a central IT organization, whether that be an in-house IT function or an outsourced provider.

This is something that is much more prevalent in the age of cloud software-as-a-service (SaaS) subscription products, as whereas in years gone by any software would have needed to be installed on the user's PC and often on a local server too, now, most software just lives in our web browsers and can be accessed anywhere.

Shadow IT is a risk as it means that data owned by your business is ending up in tools you don't control; you don't necessarily know where it is, you can't easily retrieve it, you may not be able to prevent access by former employees once they've left, and it may not be protected particularly well by the provider.

Have any of your employees signed up for ChatGPT Plus to help them with their work? This is a type of shadow IT in the AI age.

Not all process issues create risk in this way. Sometimes the issue is just inefficiency. An option gets added that comes up so rarely no one knows how to process it. Or we upgrade one system that is part of a process and not another and suddenly something that used to work well takes more time and creates more frustration for the team involved.

Managers have a lot of options to mitigate the potential for broken processes in addition to just asking team members to share them. These can include job shadowing, observation, audits, remedial training, and even appearing on the popular TV show *Undercover Boss*. But technology also offers solutions to better understand work processes and advising on fixes. Such techniques can be useful in finding opportunities to make improvements with technology, including AI technology, on a deeper, more specific, and more customized level, than just rolling out a generally capable tool like Microsoft 365 Copilot.

Process Mining is a feature of Power Automate which is part of Microsoft Power Platform, allowing those with low-code maker capabilities, to integrate real process step data with intelligent recommendations on where to focus automation activities, including AI tooling. This can be based on analyzing log data from systems of record like your finance platform (this is called data mining), or, interestingly, by recording the actions an individual worker takes to complete a task on their PC and then aggregating that data from many workers to audit deviations in how processes are completed.

Increasingly these types of tools that let you peer under the hood of how work gets done in your business are enhanced with AI to make remediating problems easier. In Process Mining for example, a Copilot attached to that product can make recommendations about automations or apps that could be built in Power Platform to make the process easier. It can then go as far as to provide you with a working template for that automation or app for you to further refine and then evaluate.

Delving deeply into this technology is beyond the scope of this chapter and this book, but it's important for you to understand that generalized tools like Microsoft 365 Copilot only meet the needs of some processes, but beyond that there is intelligent tooling you can deploy to help you identify what additional capabilities you need, and then allow you to plan either to build them using low-code, or buy a third-party app. There are other toolsets out there that offer similar functionality, but Microsoft's is particularly well integrated and focused on giving powerful capabilities with a shallow learning curve.

It may seem paradoxical to consider AI tools in helping you plan the rollout of AI in your business, but thinking back to chapter 2, we learned the range of different AI capabilities that exist, and how these might be applied to various use cases. In Microsoft's Copilot approach it has developed tools that help you in the backend and in planning, and those that are front-and-center with your team members every day.

Just as on an airplane, the copilot isn't just there for the flight, but to help plan it out ahead of time, so is the case for the Copilot tools you see in products like Process Mining or Power Apps in Microsoft's suite of products.

Action Steps

- Design a stakeholder engagement and information gathering process that's appropriate, in terms of included parties and scope, for what you are aiming to roll out and where.

- If you have complex repeatable processes that are beyond the scope of a general productivity focused AI tool like Microsoft 365 Copilot, consider investigating process mining or similar as a means to gather information that will help with targeting AI-enabled automations or apps.

7. Preparing Your Workforce: HR Strategies for the AI Era

Navigating the direct and indirect impacts of AI on your workforce should be an imperative concern for all business leaders during this period of transition.

In previous chapters we have considered the immediate concerns you may have in guiding and leading your team through AI adoption, and the concerns your employees may express about this process, but the broader impact across a plethora of people-centric or HR issues goes well beyond the boundaries of your leadership of your immediate team.

From hiring, through to AI involvement in work product, to ethical considerations, this is a technical change that will have far reaching impacts on your business in areas that have traditionally been well beyond technology considerations. Some impacts may even be felt even if you don't directly implement AI technology in your business, but as a secondary impact of AI technology being available to the wider population.

Hiring in the AI Era

The advent of AI is significantly transforming the hiring landscape, introducing new complexities for both employers and job seekers. Today's job seekers can leverage AI to their advantage, using generative AI tools like ChatGPT to enhance their job applications and resumes. These tools can create highly customized and targeted job applications at a previously unimaginable pace and scale, adding another layer of sophistication to the job seeking process. This AI-assisted job hunting not only challenges traditional hiring practices but also puts pressure on recruiters to discern between the true capabilities of a candidate and the AI-enhanced portrayal of their skills and experiences. It also potentially opens the floodgates for the volume of applications to increase as it becomes easier for jobseekers to create highly targeted, good quality applications quickly. This highlights the necessity for hiring managers, their HR specialist partners, and recruiters to familiarize themselves with these AI tools and to develop strategies to effectively evaluate AI-enhanced applications.

Already, we are seeing specialist AI platforms springing up that play directly to this jobseeker market. In one example the platform was as simple as uploading a resume and a job description, and the system could produce in seconds a fully customized job application. This makes ChatGPT look like an inefficient tool for this type of work and removes the barrier on the jobseeker of even knowing how to write a prompt that would get the output they are looking for. While jobseekers might rejoice at tools like this, for recruitment professionals the more likely response might be a groan.

In the current era, Applicant Tracking Systems (ATS) play a pivotal role in recruitment. These systems help businesses manage the recruitment process by tracking applications and offering a centralized database for candidate information. In some cases, these types of systems have offered the first glimpses to a business of how AI technology might transform their working processes. However, AI has the potential still to significantly enhance these systems, offering capabilities such as predictive analytics to figure out candidate suitability, natural language processing to understand resumes beyond mere keywords, and even machine learning algorithms to continually improve the recruitment process based on historical data.

The AI Content Identification Challenge

It is not clear that either with the AI technology we are currently using, or that which will come, there will be any foolproof way to consistently identify AI generated outputs versus that created by humans.

As AI becomes more sophisticated, in generating not just text, but also images, video, and audio, including people's voices, obvious signals that the content is AI generated have reduced to, or near, zero.

Even AI systems themselves are unable to reliably detect AI generated product. OpenAI shut down its own efforts to build systems to do this in 2023, and other fledgling operations promising to do the same have experienced unreliable results.

While there are not yet universally agreed standards on the marking of AI generated content, businesses like Microsoft, OpenAI, and Google, have taken their own approaches in technology and policy on how to go about this. For example, images from OpenAI's DALL-E image generating tool will be cryptographically tagged as having been generated by AI so that other software systems can identify them as such.

There are also concepts that have been developed on marking AI generated text, such as deploying a new set of Unicode characters (the descriptors of the letters themselves) to highlight that content versus what is written by humans.

One thing is clear though: Whether through self-regulation or governmentally imposed rules, we can imagine that the big players previously mentioned will err on the side of "safe AI" and seek to flag AI generated content whenever possible. But, as with everything else, there will be other players that will not make such efforts and will benefit from breaking the rules.

The Pandora's box of AI content is now open, and it's likely that a foolproof method to identify it will be out of our grasp for some time to come and may never actually come to fruition.

With these advancements, hiring considerations need to evolve. Businesses now need to seek out candidates who not only possess relevant industry skills but also understand how to make most effective use of AI technologies in their day-to-day work to be most productive. We can add this need for AI literacy to our existing priority for tech-literate candidates, but it's important to understand that, particularly in the context of how AI technology like Microsoft 365 Copilot will function, it will be far easier to hire someone with exemplary industry knowledge and develop their AI skills than the reverse. Being able to deliver a high quality but AI crafted job application will probably never be a useful metric for candidate suitability, particularly if that AI generated content serves to unreasonably stretch the truth or just to game the ATS.

Despite the potential benefits, the integration of AI in recruitment also raises concerns about fairness and bias. Businesses must exercise caution when considering AI in recruitment, either from the perspective of a candidate's use of AI or its integration into a company's recruitment tools, ensuring that the process remains equitable and unbiased. For example, should an AI generated application be seen as a negative, or should it be seen as the difference between sending a handwritten cover letter and one that is professionally typed? Is machine learning helpful to recruitment, or does it amplify existing biases that have been unintentionally normalized in your hiring practices? For every answer AI might give, it also has the potential to raise at least as many questions.

One of the greatest challenges for any business is attracting the right talent. AI offers up opportunities to enhance how we approach this challenge, but also presents areas where caution should be advised. Familiarity with AI and its impacts on recruitment should be an essential foundation for all hiring managers and recruiters, and it's important to be cognizant of the fact that to some extent AI technology probably already plays a role in your recruitment processes. Looking for candidates with a level of AI familiarity and comfort with these technologies is important, but savvy businesses will grapple with the fact that AI's reach into your hiring strategies goes well beyond the skills and interests of your candidates, and into the core of how your recruitment processes work and the scale they need to operate at.

Employee Development for the AI Age

As AI becomes integral to our business operations, employee development strategies need to evolve to meet the demands of this new era.

Developing a workforce that not only understands AI but can also effectively use it for business advantage is of paramount importance. This requires a multi-faceted approach that combines technical skill development, cultivation of an AI-ready mindset, and a strong understanding of AI ethics and the potential biases inherent in AI systems. It's also vital to maintain momentum around the cultural perspective of AI to ensure it is viewed positively by team members.

If deploying a tool like Microsoft 365 Copilot, its connectivity with your existing productivity tools means the effort in technical training versus deploying something completely new may be reduced. But it's important to not forget that while this may just seem to be an extra capability in Microsoft Word, it's also a fundamentally novel technology that requires some foundational understanding to use effectively.

Microsoft supplies a robust adoption framework for most of its tools, and this includes its Copilot products. While these frameworks are predominantly focused on achieving certain goals through technical means, there is a big component of the people side of such adoptions. As such you have a ready to use set of information and tools tailored to the software products you have decided to deploy in your business, where your technical teams, communications specialists, and those focused on people development can come together to build robust adoption programs. Similarly, Google has resources to help with these purposes as do most major software vendors in this space.

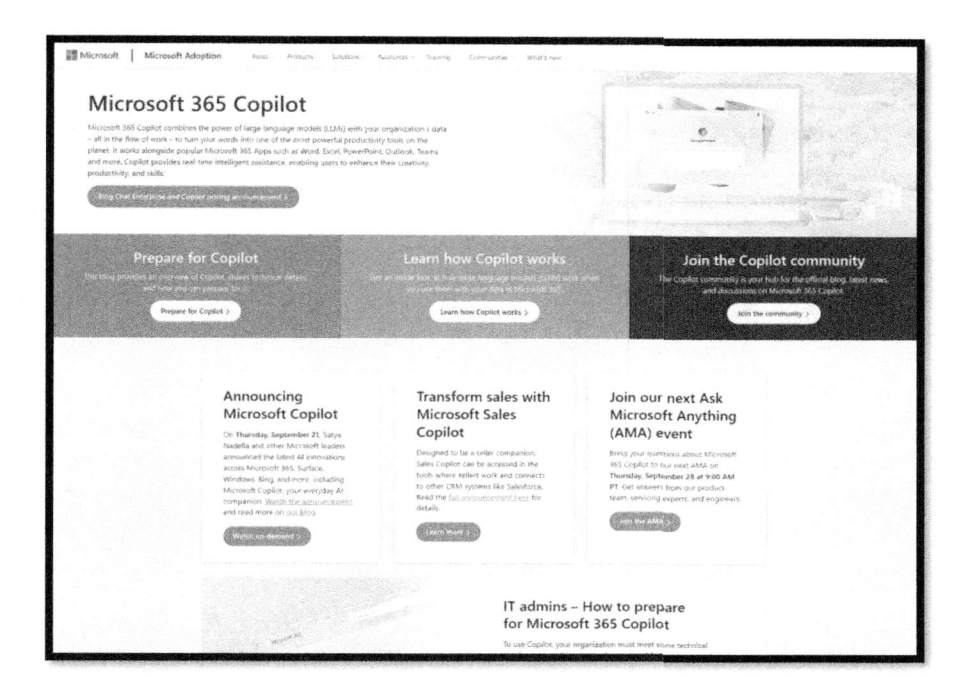

Figure 4: The homepage of Microsoft's Copilot Adoption website in September 2023.

Continuous learning will be a cornerstone of employee development through the infancy of our AI era. The technology will continue to constantly evolve, and one of the biggest challenges will be ensuring that employees are keeping pace, not just with the technical challenges like making data accessible, but also the non-technical issues like ethics.

As AI systems become more prevalent in decision-making processes, employees need to be aware of the ethical implications. Training programs should, therefore, include modules on AI ethics, covering topics such as data privacy, fairness, and transparency. It is vital that employees understand the types of mistakes that AI tools can make when generating content and what underlies those mistakes. This topic is covered in more detail in chapter 8.

The New AI Career: Prompt Engineering

The most positive forecast of the impact AI will have on jobs, and one that is evidenced in previous technological advances, is that new, unimagined jobs will appear that start to replace any that are less in demand because of the technology.

One such new job has appeared already, that of Prompt Engineer.

A Prompt Engineer is an expert in crafting the inputs we give to the large language model to allow it to give the best possible response most accurately. The key skills here are being able to understand how different types of input impact the generated response, and how to deploy this knowledge in various business contexts to drive interactions with the AI.

This is exactly the type of role individuals who take part in your AI adoption might start to glide towards if you focus on building the right technical and non-technical skills around the technology. Murial in your accounting department might have absolutely zero prior interest in AI or technology but find that she's just really great crafting prompts that get high quality and consistent responses that can be used across your business.

There are likely to be other new roles that arrive due to our exploration of AI, and this might mark an exciting possibility for employees who are otherwise concerned about its impact on the jobs they do.

For its part, Microsoft's own communications about its Microsoft 365 Copilot capabilities have been plain in stating that a copilot is there to help you develop a first draft, and not a final product, and this understanding must be foundational for all your employees. However, it is possible that unintended biases exist in your data, or there are perspectives that have been shared in the past that are not your current thinking that could be exposed by a copilot's capabilities – getting ahead of these issues so that your employees understand what the AI is doing, and what it is not, is essential.

By equipping employees with the right skills, ethical understanding, and mindset, businesses can harness the full potential of AI and deploy copilots that help their teams maintain their competitive edge.

Why Generative AI Hallucinates

Throughout this book we have referred to using AI tools to "draft" rather than "write" content, and in chapter 9 we will dig deeply into how to sense check AI responses.

The reality is that while generative AI is amazing it's also frequently wrong. Not necessarily in how it writes or how it draws conclusions, but in how it connects, or just imagines or hallucinates facts that don't really exist.

A tool like ChatGPT or Microsoft 365 Copilot isn't really a writer, not in the human sense, it's more a sophisticated probability calculator. It "understands" based solely on the likelihood that certain words follow others based upon its training on huge amounts of written data.

It's likely to be able to tell you that Charles III is the King of England, but sometimes it might imagine that Felix the Cat is the King of England, and it will be just as confident in writing that into a response as the right answer. And without digging into everything it's trained on, neither the user nor those who built the AI will ever know where that wrong answer came from.

When AI is generating text based on topics you know well this isn't such an issue, but if you're relying on it to generate responses on topics you don't know at all, it can be problematic.

This is why for now, and for some time to come, the ideal use case for generative AI is to help you speed up or improve a task you would already be doing. It provides the draft, you review it with some existing expertise on the topic, and you can decide it's good to go. Outside of this workflow, hallucinations can be dangerous and should be carefully monitored.

Building HR Policies for AI-related Concerns

As AI becomes more integrated in the workplace, it is crucial for businesses to review their HR and work policies to ensure the right considerations are in place for governing its use. These policies should provide clear guidelines on how AI can and should be used within the organization, ensuring its use is ethical, responsible, and aligned with the company's values.

Even if you are not currently rolling out the use of AI within your business, shoring up your policies in relation to the AI capabilities that are available to your team members outside your approved business systems is essential. In many cases this may simply mean adding some specific AI-related considerations to policy standards you already have in place.

Protecting your data should be a primary concern. AI systems rely upon vast amounts of data to function, and you have probably been collecting the various datasets that tools like Microsoft 365 Copilot will use to leverage benefit for many years. However, being clear about what data you collect, how it's stored, how it's used, and how you protect it, is essential. There are two specific areas here that are worth digging into in the context of AI.

Many businesses are somewhat poor at ensuring that data is only preserved for its stated and approved uses. Pressing delete on that 10-year-old customer data can just feel wrong, no matter how many policies state that you shouldn't have it, and how aware you are that it probably is no longer useful. This type of data hoarding is something we see in many small businesses, and as our ability to collect data grows, so does the problem. But, in the context of a product like Microsoft 365 Copilot, it doesn't have the nuanced understanding you do that the folder of old data is there as a security blanket, not for active use - it either has access to data or it doesn't. So suddenly, you are not just holding onto data just in case, you have tools that are actively using data, perhaps in a way that is against your existing policies or compliance needs, or even just drawing the wrong conclusions by relying on out-of-date information. You must have policies around how data should be used, but you also must ensure those policies are alive in your organization in how you use and curate your data day-to-day. For some, compliance standards like GDPR (more on this in chapter 8) will mandate that you have the correct lifecycle for your data, for others this is simply good practice, but in the age of AI, it's an essential for everyone.

Protection of data should be another area where you really think about how your policies may be impacted by AI technology. There was a recent news story where workers associated with Samsung decided to use ChatGPT for work purposes. They ended up using proprietary company information in their requests, and anyone who has used ChatGPT should be aware that OpenAI places no prohibition on its ability to use the content of those requests for further training of its systems. So, essentially, those workers shared their company's proprietary secrets with anyone who might make a request to ChatGPT. Like this context, even if you are not rolling out AI technology within your organization, you need policies to control its use on your behalf by workers through the requests they may make to AI services they have access to. If you already have policies to stop your team members sending company information through their personal email accounts, you may need to enhance these for the AI age by also deciding how you balance a worker's ability to use the best tooling against your need to control the flow of your data. If you use Microsoft 365, even if you are not going to deploy a tool like Microsoft 365 Copilot, you can opt to use Bing Chat Enterprise, which at present is the only AI chat tool connected to search that promises to respect the security of your company's information.

Understanding Data Compliance Technology

A core part of the Microsoft 365 offering is data compliance, and as you enhance your tooling with higher level licenses like Microsoft 365 Business Premium or E5, the sophistication of the tools you have access to increases.

Diving deep on this technology is beyond the scope of this book but it's important to understand, both for technology leaders, and leaders in other areas like HR, that there are technology-based tools in the major vendors' productivity suites that can help you turn your policies into guardrails.

Foundationally, an effective data governance strategy should consist of more than just policies, to help ensure compliance and give effective support to your team members to do the right thing when it comes to data.

Tools like Data Loss Prevention (DLP) policies, Sensitivity Labels, and Access Reviews can be effective in ensuring your policies are turned into practice.

An effective control that exists for all licenses and across the products of different vendors is data access controls. Ensuring each user has just enough access for the job they are doing prevents situations where they inadvertently use or share data they shouldn't. An added benefit here is that because a tool like Microsoft 365 Copilot works in the security context of the user, if you ensure your users only have access to data they should be using, you prevent your AI tool from relying on data that shouldn't be used.

Outside of issues related to your data, you need to consider how you deliver transparency in the context of AI. If you deploy Microsoft 365 Copilot, how should it be used and how should that use be flagged to others? Is it okay for your team members to submit work that was essentially generated by AI? If that's okay internally, how about when it comes to client work? Even if you have these policies, how do you police them, and how do you integrate information related to them in reviewing employee performance? And, beyond the individual worker, you have the issue of transparency on a business-wide basis around how AI is used, and if you use your own customized technologies, what data is used in their training. These issues of transparency and honesty are at the heart of many of the ethical considerations in using AI.

Policies that address the possibility of bias in the use of AI, either in how processes make use of the tools, or in the underlying data they rely upon are extremely important. As AI tools have developed, so have unexpected biases, not placed there intentionally but through having data that isn't representative of the truth, or by making assumptions that apply a result to one group but not another. Facial recognition is a notable example of how such biases can play out, and particularly where such tools are used in contexts such as policing can have unwanted and dangerous impacts. Companies like Microsoft have sought to eliminate this potential as far as possible in products like Microsoft 365 Copilot by wrapping your data and requests in meta-prompts that guide the AI in how to eliminate biased responses, but you should still institute policies that guide team members on how to avoid biased implementations and how to flag up instances of bias they may be seeing in the use of AI tools in your business.

By setting up comprehensive and clear AI-related HR policies, businesses can create a framework for responsible AI use within the organization. These policies can help to prevent misuse of AI technologies, protect employee rights, treat customers fairly, and ensure that AI is used in a manner that is beneficial for both the organization and its team members.

HR Ethics for the AI Age

As AI becomes more deeply integrated into the workplace, ethical considerations become increasingly important. In chapter 8 we will look specifically at several ethics issues that are relevant to the intersection of AI and human resources and the unique ethical challenges that businesses must address to maintain trust and integrity in their operations.

Fairness, which we will explore more generally later, should be a primary ethical consideration when using AI in HR. AI systems can unintentionally perpetuate or amplify biases present in the data they rely upon and on which they are trained, which can result in unfair outcomes in areas such as recruitment, and performance evaluation.

Similarly, privacy and transparency are issues we will explore in greater detail, but as specifically linked to HR, it is essential that employees know when AI is being used and trust that their privacy will be maintained.

As we have already highlighted, when it comes to systems like Microsoft 365 Copilot, a key consideration should be your data hygiene, but if you choose to deploy AI in other areas, such as with ATS software, then truly understanding what sort of datasets have been used to train those tools, and how they interface with your historic data, should be essential to give all parties confidence in their use.

With respect to Microsoft's AI tools specifically, including Microsoft 365 Copilot, there is a clear line drawn between the data it can use to train its models and your business data. Your data is only used in the context of that which any given user has existing access to, and your requests or associated data are never used for training or related purposes. However, as we have already learned, each provider of similar AI tools has different standards when it comes to the retention and use of your data. It's vital that you take the time to understand how the software vendor might use your data and whether it will be utilized in the future for model training that could expose it to others outside your organization.

In conclusion, ethics must be at the forefront of HR in the age of AI. By considering fairness, transparency, privacy, and associated issues like respecting autonomy, businesses can ensure that their use of AI in HR is ethical and responsible. By putting these considerations at the center of any AI adoption, you help to mitigate the very human concerns your employees may have around this fast-evolving technology and maximize the potential for it to bring benefits both to your business and to the lives of your team members.

Action Items

- Review your employee handbook or other employee policies to ensure that expectations connected to the use of AI, including sharing company data with outside AI systems, are clear.

- Consider additional processes, training, or tools to address AI generated job applications appearing as part of recruitment for vacant roles.

- Take your data governance seriously. This is an issue whether you use AI or not, but in the age of AI existing weaknesses may be further exposed. Consider implementing data compliance tooling to solidify your policies into practice.

8. AI and Privacy: Navigating Legal and Ethical Considerations

As our new AI copilots help us to guide our work more efficiently toward our chosen destinations, their integration into our processes can give rise to questions about exactly how they are working and how they are using data to do their job. The rise of the Internet over the last few decades, and then, more recently, social media, has made issues of privacy a front-and-center topic for many, and these concerns are rightly even more amplified as we step into the new AI era.

AI is revolutionizing, and will continue to revolutionize, various aspects of our lives, from the way we communicate and work, to how we make decisions and solve complex problems. These transformational changes come with questions about privacy, ethics, and fairness that must be answered for us to feel assured that they are delivering benefits to our lives. As AI systems become more sophisticated and pervasive, the need to consider and address these issues becomes increasingly critical.

The intersection of AI technology with the issue of privacy is one that deserves significant attention. AI systems bring new types of capacity and capability to the collection, processing, and analysis of vast datasets, which in many cases may include or be focused on personal data. These tools can work at unprecedented speed and scale, opening new avenues for innovation, but also potential new privacy concerns. How do we ensure that AI is used responsibly and ethically? And how can we balance the benefits we are trying to deliver with AI with the need for personal privacy protections?

In the coming sections we will explore aspects of the legal and regulatory landscape that surrounds AI. This, like this entire book, is designed to be informational and not legal advice to be relied upon by your business. Just as AI technology is rapidly evolving, so is the picture around regulation and compliance best practices.

Foundationally organizations must establish transparency, accountability, and sufficient governance practices around their use of AI. However, these standards should simply build upon existing frameworks that are in place for current uses of personal data, as the impetus to protect the privacy of employees and customers is certainly not new. Like so many of the points we have looked at in this book so far, AI gives us the opportunity to polish and refine what we should have already been doing, rather than creating a wholly distinct set of challenges set apart from the existing best practice standards.

What is privacy in the context of AI?

Privacy is broadly regarded as a fundamental right we all have, but one that has been increasingly challenged in the Internet age through the growth of data collection, the propensity for data breaches, and the connection between highly targeted advertising and the profits large tech businesses rely upon.

The United Nations Universal Declaration of Human Rights outlines privacy as part of Article 12:

"No one shall be subjected to arbitrary interference with his privacy, family, home or correspondence, nor to attacks upon his honour and reputation. Everyone has the right to the protection of the law against such interference or attacks."

This document was not published with AI or even the challenges of Internet technology in mind when it was approved by the UN General Assembly in 1948. However, standards such as these are just as relevant, if not more so, as we embark into the AI age.

Over the course of our development of Internet technology, our understanding of what constitutes privacy has evolved and expanded. New regulatory measures have been introduced to explicitly define and protect this fundamental right, such as the General Data Protection Regulation (GDPR) in Europe and the California Consumer Privacy Act (CCPA) in the United States.

The GDPR, introduced by the European Union in 2018, set out a robust framework for the protection of personal data. It emphasizes the principles of data minimization, purpose limitation, and accountability. It also establishes the rights of individuals to understand, access, and, in some cases, delete their personal data held by organizations.

These principles have a profound impact on AI systems. AI and machine learning models often rely on vast amounts of data for training and decision-making. Under GDPR, the data collected must be minimal and used solely for the purpose stated, requiring a considered approach to the design and deployment of AI systems. Furthermore, GDPR's "right to explanation" gives individuals the right to understand the logic, significance, and consequences of automated decisions made about them. This includes decisions made by AI, effectively making the issue of being able to track back the rationale for AI generated decisions a legal obligation.

The CCPA, which was enacted in 2020, grants a broadly similar set of rights about personal data related to the state of California. Like GDPR, it brings issues of transparency to the forefront, requiring clarity from businesses on how they collect or use personal data, which would include data used to train or run AI systems.

Compliance with such regulations should not just be about avoiding enforcement and potential penalties, but about showing respect for the fundamental right everyone has to personal privacy. As AI continues to advance, becoming more integrated into our lives, this respect for privacy should be a crucial element in ensuring the technology is used for societal benefit while protecting individuals, but also giving businesses the chance for greater levels of success.

For the part of current AI development companies, since the introduction of ChatGPT, several have been involved in discussions about potential industry-wide regulation. The focus of this discussion has not necessarily been privacy, but it does form an important aspect of the reasons why greater regulation may be needed for the industry, now and in the future.

The Role of AI Users in Privacy

For businesses rolling out products like Microsoft 365 Copilot the full weight of the imperative for AI systems to work with privacy in mind does not fall on your organization but is shared between you and your provider.

In the specific case of Microsoft's copilot product, it is built on top of a Microsoft-hosted version of OpenAI's GPT large language model. The training data for these models has not been publicly released, so while experts have been able to infer what that training dataset might consist of, we cannot know conclusively everything the model is trained on. This is counter to the assertion that AI use should be transparent, but one rationale given by OpenAI of this limitation of its transparency is to avoid privacy risks. In addition to OpenAI's commitments, Microsoft has its own set of responsible AI standards governing its data use.

Within the context of using Microsoft 365 Copilot in your Microsoft 365 tenant, your data remains your data and Microsoft expresses a strong and long-term commitment to this operating principle. This means that through using these tools, your data is not shared with any outside organization (including OpenAI), and your data and prompts are never used to enhance or train the underlying model. A similar set of commitments exists relating to Microsoft's other AI powered products including any use you make of Azure Cognitive Services or the Azure OpenAI Service to build your own AI supported technologies.

If you use a platform other than Microsoft 365 Copilot then you need to be sure that you fully understand how that platform will use your data; and you should also understand that the terms around Microsoft's products might change over time, so you should keep on top of any changes in the terms of service of the products you use.

However, just because your service provider offers commitments around their ethical use of AI and how they protect your data, doesn't mean that you should feel as if you are off the hook in building out your own policies, procedures and commitments that reinforce privacy and ethics in your AI use.

Data retention and access should be important issues in any business holding customer data, but any problems in those areas can be amplified by the way AI tools can work to reinforce and augment your operations.

In the context of Microsoft 365 Copilot for example, you can ask the service to generate new content based upon existing data you have access to. Your request is coupled with data to allow it to be delivered based solely on the access you have based on your user. If you have access to the wrong data, or too much data, or to records that should have been deleted and no longer used, Microsoft 365 Copilot doesn't know, it only sees what you have access to based upon searching your accessible files in relation to the request you have made.

Correcting this problem is one of having proper data governance, access controls, and retention standards within your organization, as outlined in chapter 7. None of these issues are specifically linked to deploying AI, but for the reasons outlined above, any deficiencies here can potentially come into sharp focus and be amplified in the context of using AI tools.

Broader ethical considerations

While privacy is extremely important, it is certainly not the only ethical issue that can be raised in using AI. As a business leader, you must take responsibility for ensuring that your use of AI is broadly and legally ethical, but also ethical in terms of the underlying values of your organization.

Frameworks like UNESCO's *"Recommendation on the Ethics of Artificial Intelligence"*, which was published in 2021, outline the breadth of the potential ethical issues that arise using AI which go well beyond the treatment of data and respect of privacy.

One major area of ethical concern is bias. AI systems can unintentionally perpetuate or amplify biases present in their training data or algorithms. A clear example of this arose in 2018 when Amazon had to scrap an AI recruiting tool after finding it unintentionally discriminated against women. The system was trained on historical hiring data that reflected male-dominated applicant pools, thereby embedding gender bias into its selections.

Situations like this highlight why it is vital to proactively audit AI systems for unwanted bias. Diversity and inclusion should be core principles governing your use of AI. Leaders must ensure they have ethical oversight processes to identify any biases before they lead to unfair impacts on employees or customers.

It is also important to consider that examples like this almost always reflect actions that unintentionally and unknowingly create bias. If your office is full of men, it might be because your business purposefully seeks to exclude women, but more likely that over time aspects of your recruiting process, from how you advertise positions, to how flexible your terms are, to the culture in your spaces have advantaged men in unplanned ways. We must be open to identifying and correcting such biases without feeling they are a repudiation of the unintentional actions that led to them. Some past actions were egregious and deserving of being highlighted, but in many cases were not, and the important thing is to correct them in the now, so they do not perpetuate into the future.

There is also a need to be thoughtful about the period over which your data has been gathered. If in the last two years your business has invested heavily in DEI (Diversity, Equity, and Inclusion) efforts that is helping you to see more diversity in your team, but at the same time you build out an AI tool to help you filter job applications that is based on the previous 10-years of data, then it's likely these two efforts will be working, at least to some extent, in opposite directions. The data may be useful, but you must ensure that it does not include out-of-date intentions or understandings that have helped to build the biases you might now be looking to address.

Transparency is another key ethical imperative. You should inform users when an AI system is involved in decisions that affect them. Providing clear explanations of the data and logic behind AI-assisted choices builds understanding and trust. This is a major drive currently in the AI industry as for a long time it has been accepted that the AI models are essentially locked boxes through which we cannot understand the logic of what is being produced. In many areas of work that impact people this is simply insufficient, and an increasing focus in boosting the efficacy and trust of AI tools generally is to be better at having those tools show their work and describe the steps they went through to reach their conclusion.

Ultimately, responsible leaders must weigh the benefits against any potential downsides before deploying AI. Partnering with experts in AI ethics can help assess where there are risks that undermine principles of fairness, accountability, and transparency. With proper governance, AI can be channeled positively, but we must be vigilant against its misuse.

For those seeking to adopt tools like Microsoft 365 Copilot instead of building AI tools from scratch there is the huge advantage of having a company with the scale and scope of Microsoft invested in these sorts of issues for their tools. Responsible AI is at the core of Microsoft's approach to building AI capabilities, looking out for ethical issues is built into their fabric, and through adoption support that learns from the experiences of many businesses, you have a best-in-class roadmap to prepare your organization to benefit from this technology while minimizing your exposure to its downsides.

The copilot sitting next to you in the cockpit must be supervised and you must build the right guardrails to ensure it is helping you in a way that aligns with your aims and values. Ultimately, the output of these tools will come down to the work we do as pilots to guide them toward the types of outputs we want.

Action Steps

- Consider how your business approaches privacy. Are there any legal frameworks like GDPR that apply to you (it applies to more organizations than just those based in Europe)? Review your current standards.

- How do the ethical considerations around AI align with the values of your business? Think about how you can update assets like your organizational vision to consider the needs of an AI-enabled world.

9. The Role of AI in Decision-Making and Data Analysis

Using AI tools to better analyze data and to make sounder decisions resulting from that analysis is an important routine use case that can be applied in almost any organizational setting.

Datasets have grown far quicker than the ability most of us possess to use them effectively. Even small businesses gather mountains of data through the various systems they use; email and other communications, customer survey systems, point-of-sale systems, production management software, and timekeeping or payroll to name but a few. The default state in most software is to store a lot of data, and while tools like Power BI have grown in popularity due to their ease-of-use in building analytics, it is still often far more complex to work out what to do with data than it is to gather it in the first place.

How can AI be your copilot in your decision-making journey? And how can it help you as an analysis tool that enables you to better understand your business? What issues should you look out for as you start to use AI to help you wrangle your ever-growing stockpile of data?

Understanding AI powered data analytics

Tools like Microsoft 365 Copilot inside your business productivity software, and ChatGPT that are accessible to anyone anywhere, are potentially a democratizing force in bringing AI capabilities that were previously the domain of big corporations to every scale of business.

For many years we have heard the term "big data", describing the huge datasets that are often leveraged by large businesses using expensive enterprise-grade tooling to give them levels of insights that are difficult to grasp. Out of these innovations has come the ability of the likes of Amazon to always know what you may want to buy, or Facebook to understand what content you want to see, or YouTube to serve you exactly the right video to keep you watching hour-after-hour. In the background, many of these leaps of understanding have not only been about the ability to store massive datasets, but to use computers to make sense of them, often with tooling that uses AI and its associated machine learning capabilities.

For small businesses, the data may not be so "big", but it is no less valuable. While the scale of data collection may be orders of magnitude smaller than for those huge corporations, gaining value from data comes down to the same core capabilities of analyzing and interpreting it. AI tools can process enormous amounts of data faster than any human could, identifying patterns, trends, and relationships that are not immediately apparent. It can turn your data into an invaluable asset that helps drive decision-making and strategy and helps you to compete on a level playing field with much larger organizations.

There are several AI-powered capabilities that are useful to analyzing any dataset, and it's important that you understand this range of tools to know what is possible, and what might be going on in the background when you prompt your chosen AI tool to help you analyze your data.

Predictive analytics is the capability to take historical data and make predictions for the future based on it. For example, taking several years of your sales data to make predictions about what your sales budget should be next year or next quarter.

Clustering is the process of grouping similar data points together based on shared characteristics. An example of this might be for the purpose of customer segmentation. This can help, for instance, to make marketing more effective by allowing you to break down your audience into logical groups with different needs or interests.

Root cause analysis identifies the underlying factors contributing to problems. It digs deeper than surface symptoms to pinpoint core issues which, if addressed, could prevent repetition. For example, examining customer complaint data could uncover root causes like product design flaws.

In large part these sorts of capabilities are not new because of AI innovation. What the computer is doing in the background is simply achieving the data organization and math far quicker and at a greater scale than would reasonably be achieved by most humans. However, there are new approaches we can take to interrogating large datasets, particularly data that is qualitative and not consistently structured, that are very much AI-enabled.

An example of this is a capability like **natural language processing (NLP)** that opens doors to features like sentiment analysis. This is where you can take some text, such as a review, and work out with a high degree of probability whether the message is positive, negative or neutral. You can, for example, use this to field customer correspondence out of hours, where problems would be immediately flagged, or to analyze huge quantities of review information. This is an area where AI has provided us with new, not just quicker or more scalable, tools.

The data analysis capabilities coming to Excel with Microsoft 365 Copilot are not going to be radical or exciting to anyone who spends a lot of their time using a product like Power BI or other advanced data analytics tools already. The point is not to replace the value of specialist tools or specialist employees, but to recognize that data is becoming increasingly important to the success of many knowledge workers' jobs, and often there is an impasse in how to use available data in a way that truly adds value. A lot of potential value is locked up in Excel spreadsheets in our businesses, and creating a new tooling that allows anyone to start releasing that value using simple natural language prompts allows us to get much more benefit from data. These new capabilities will likely give more people a shallow learning curve into the world of data analytics, but that journey may well end in Power BI or other similar powerful tools as it does for many already. Outside of this, those who experience hesitancy in using an app like Excel at all, will be able to use copilot capabilities to help them navigate its features in an easy to access way, turning a sea of buttons on the ribbon into something much more user friendly, and potentially creating files that are much more useable and understandable both to colleagues and to AI tools that might be interrogating them.

Advanced Data Analysis

One of the more exciting features to be added to ChatGPT since its initial release is a capability called Advanced Data Analysis. This offers a plain natural language focused canvas from which to have AI help you carry out analytical tasks.

For example, you can take an Excel spreadsheet full of your company's financial data, upload it to ChatGPT, and ask Advanced Data Analysis to produce insights from it. It can create new tables, graphs, even new files to download, all generated by the AI model's understanding of your data and interpretation of your prompt.

This capability also provides interesting insights into how it's working by allowing you to peek at the code it's running behind the scenes to get the output you see. Essentially this service is running a Python sandbox and then generating code in Python, using various libraries accessible in that language, to complete the analysis tasks for you.

This is similar to the capabilities that will be coming to Excel through Microsoft 365 Copilot, and we do already have existing natural language to analysis capabilities in Power BI that can achieve similar results, but even so, the simple useability of Advanced Data Analysis is astounding. On the next page you can see analysis it provides on a dataset it simulated itself when simply asked "Summarize this data and provide suggestions on what it represents."

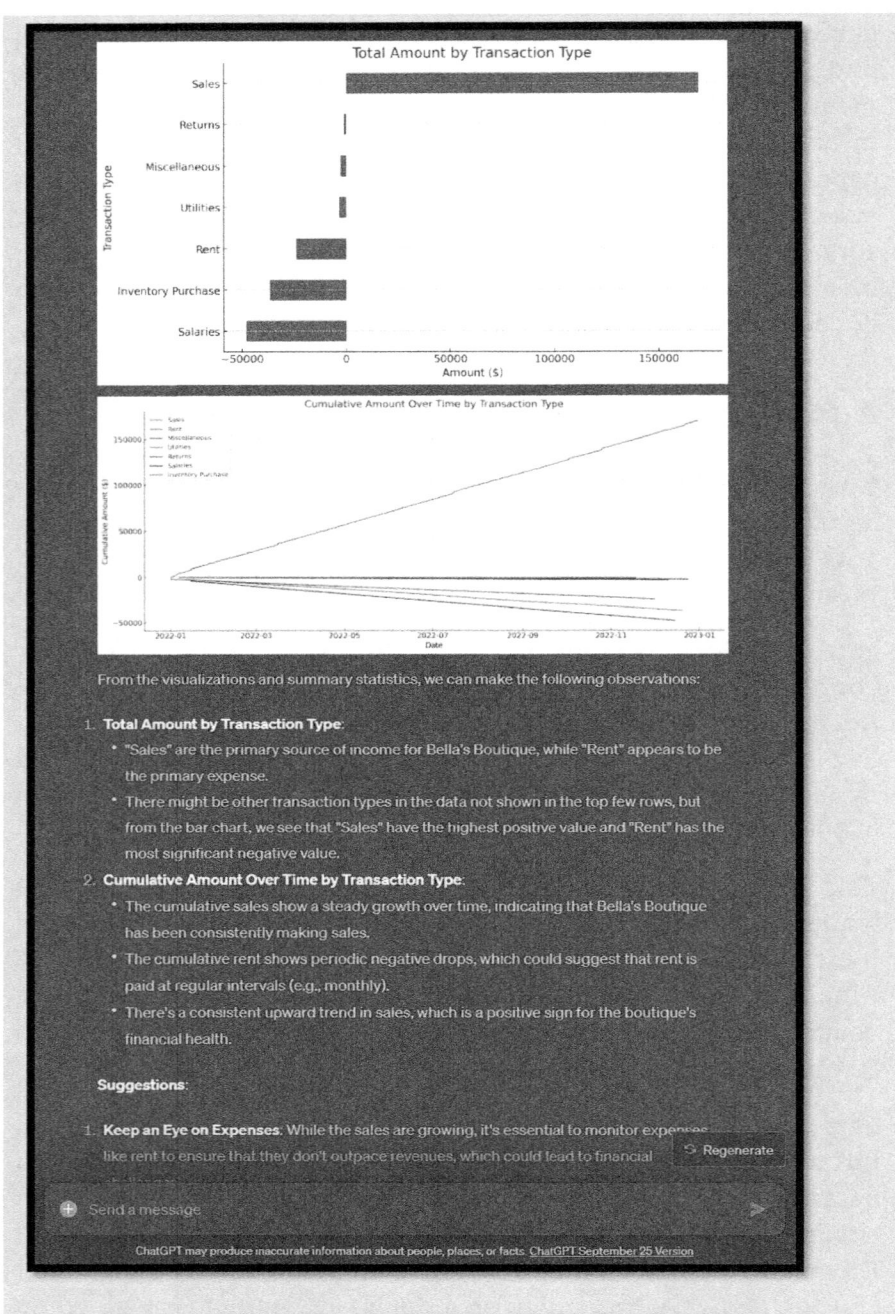

Figure 5: Example of ChatGPT's Advanced Data Analysis capabilities

It's important to continue to highlight that in all these cases, the outcome can only be as good as the data. AI is extremely capable in seeing patterns in data at a speed or volume that would be impossible for any human, but it lacks the ability that many humans would have to intuitively fill in the gaps when looking at an issue they know well but with incomplete information. Undoubtedly, with advances like GPT-4, AI is becoming better at achieving improved results, but it is still no match for a sensible and experienced human in many scenarios. As a copilot your AI tools can help you get to a satisfactory answer quickly and across a large set of data, but determining whether that answer is the right one to proceed forward with is still your role as the human pilot.

Consider the example of a small online retailer that used AI to better understand its customer behavior. By using AI tools, they could be able to segment their customers, predict future buying trends, and understand the sentiment behind customer reviews. This can enable more targeted marketing efforts and better procurement planning more aligned to the expected need for stock. AI can provide the analysis that offers those kinds of recommendations, but they should be sense checked by human workers with the right experience and skills.

How to sense check AI-driven conclusions

Establishing a reasonable approach in how to go about the process of sense checking the work product of AI is an extremely important operational step. Putting in place good practices that reasonably check the work of AI not only help to protect your business and your customers but can be demonstrative to your employees of your continued commitment to the value their unique skills and experience bring to your ability to succeed.

If you simply repeat all the work to check its right then you've gained no advantage from using AI, but if you just glance over the work without diving into the detail at all, you might miss important inaccuracies. It's important to strike the right balance, and to recognize that this balance may shift over time as you get used to where AI is most reliable for your use cases.

Each situation will be a little different based on exactly what type of analysis you are looking for, but your sense check step can consist of some common elements.

How in line is the analysis with what you think you already know? Just because the AI output aligns with your current understanding, or perhaps it is 180-degrees different, doesn't mean it's right or wrong; but the further the output deviates from what you expect, the more critical analysis you should probably consider doing. If you know over time your business' bank balance has grown, but AI analysis of your performance suggests you've made a loss every month, it deserves some detailed review.

Are there objective elements of the analysis that are easy to check for accuracy? A while back I used a new AI tool for some data analysis testing that included revenue by state. It told me there were 30 results. Given that I expected that my dataset included revenue from all 50 states, there was a high likelihood that something had gone wrong in the analysis. So, checking into what was going on, I found my data had hit the limit of how many rows the tool was able to work on, it was just missing some of the data. This certainly isn't a sure-fire way of checking the accuracy of everything, but if an analysis is clearly wrong on the basics it's not worth considering anything else.

Demonstrate efficacy on sample data. Starting small is the best strategy. You might want to analyze 10-years of sales data, but if what you're trying to do doesn't work on data for a sample week, there's little point in proceeding forward without change. The power of AI does not preclude the need to test your approach just as you would with any other technology.

Any user ignores these steps, or similar, at their peril. As time goes on, our ability to trust AI outputs, and for AI tools to explain in easily understood ways how they reached those outputs, will increase. But, with your initial steps into this technology, making reasonable efforts to sense check the work of AI as comprehensively as necessary is vital.

The Best Prompt Wins!

It's possible to automate the process of running AI-enabled tasks with software solutions such as Power Automate, so whatever task you are running is done so consistently on a certain dataset that updates on a regular basis.

However, in the context of using products like Microsoft 365 Copilot, or even ChatGPT's Advanced Data Analysis, your interaction with the technology will be based upon your natural language request – or prompt.

Some prompts are simply better than others at getting the type of information you need out of the AI tool. And it's important to understand that it's the **type** of information, not certain information, as depending on what you are asking for the AI model may, even with the same data and prompt, provide a slightly different response each time.

Creating good prompts, and then reusing those prompts across your business for certain tasks, will be as important in the future as documenting and consistently delivering other processes today. There will be certain steps to take to get AI to do its best work, just as there are certain established processes in a restaurant of how orders get relayed to a kitchen for a chef to be able to deliver the best food to customers.

Microsoft has established its own strategy connected to this issue by building a tool called Copilot Lab that will be available to Microsoft 365 Copilot users to enable them to share prompts and prompting best practices across their organization. Equally, with the release of its own enterprise-focused tier of tool, ChatGPT Enterprise, OpenAI added a feature to allow prompts to be shared on an organization-wide basis.

AI assisted decision-making.

AI has significant potential to enhance data-driven decision making across a range of business functions. In sales, AI systems can rapidly analyze customer data to identify the most promising prospects for campaigns. In HR, predictive algorithms can surface top candidates from applicant pools. However, leaders should implement AI carefully, not handing full control to machines.

For example, an AI tool may identify that targeting younger consumers has historically correlated with higher sales. But leaders need to look beyond the data, considering whether age-based marketing aligns with company values, or perhaps risks alienating existing customers. Compliance risks around discrimination also need evaluation. While AI can process massive amounts of data quickly, human judgment is vital to add color and flavor to the directions we choose to take.

In the AI world, the term alignment is used to consider to what extent a tool or model is aligned with human ethics and values. In the 2003 paper *"Ethical Issues in Advanced Artificial Intelligence"*, the philosopher, Nick Bostrom wrote about the paperclip maximizer thought experiment. This considered an advanced AI given the sole job of making as many paperclips as possible. With this single task, it could quickly conclude that it would be able to achieve this goal much better with Earth just turned into a paperclip manufacturing facility. This, clearly, highlights a very capable AI tool that was very poorly aligned with human values.

While no one is suggesting that any of today's AI tools are capable of eliminating our home planet in the search for paperclips, this concept can help to create understanding as to why AI-supported data analysis turning into AI-powered decision-making should be seen as a non-trivial step. As humans there are lots of values-based and ethics-driven shortcuts we take in communicating our intentions to those around us. For example, in a workplace setting, I've never felt the need to explicitly instruct an employee not to physically harm our customers, it's just a given. But without human ethics, an instruction such as "Do all you can to avoid anyone leaving a negative review", could turn very dark very quickly.

Effective AI alignment involves humans setting goals, parameters, and guardrails to guide the technology. Leaders must critically evaluate AI recommendations, questioning the data sources, weighing ethical factors, and supplementing with diverse human perspectives before acting. The human supervision imperative means that for some time to come we may focus on AI-assisted or AI-supported decision making rather than decisions that are entirely driven and executed by AI. There has been much talk in the press about the concept of AI CEOs being on the horizon, but until issues like these are resolved, ideas such as this are overblown and fanciful.

This is the area where Microsoft's Copilot branding tells us the most about the technologies it is building. In a pilot's and copilot's relationship the roles and hierarchies are clear; even if a copilot spends much of their time flying the plane autonomously, the work they do is ultimately supervised by and the responsibility of the pilot. It's easy to consider these AI Copilots just in the sense of being an assisting force, but we must not forget that this monicker also implies a responsibility on the human as the leader and supervisor. These tools are here to augment, not replace, and in no type of role is this more important than in making decisions that will impact our lives, our businesses, or the wellbeing of those involved with them. While such a concept has not yet been tested legally, it's unlikely a defense of "The AI decided to do that" after some accident or disaster would stand up to scrutiny.

For example, before implementing an AI-suggested pricing change, leaders should review the competitive landscape, customer sentiment, and potential long-term brand impacts. Doing this all before rolling out adjustments based solely on an algorithmic output. The data the AI has considered should be known, and the logic it has utilized to reach its decision should be checked.

Imagine asking an AI to decide who should be laid off. Or what business units should be closed. Or even who would be a suitable candidate to receive some expensive medical treatment. The future is potentially awash with decisions we might want AI to help us with where the ethics hurdles are in stark focus from the outset.

There is an important other side to this issue though, and that comes back to unintended bias. Humans are biased, mostly unconsciously, but biased all the same. If who is going to receive an expensive medical treatment should be an entirely objective decision, then a well-designed data-driven machine is potentially significantly more capable than the average human, but the right AI tool for this is unlikely to be the generative language models that are the focus of our attention here. For this reason, these are incredibly complex and nuanced issues.

When thinking about Microsoft's Copilot products, we must remember that consideration of these issues is placed for us both in plain sight and hidden behind the scenes. In plain sight are warnings highlighting that AI outputs might be wrong. Behind the scenes are Microsoft's meta-prompts that guide the AI in how it responds to your prompts no matter what you type. This means that even if you try hard to goad the machine into generating a misaligned response, you're going to have an uphill battle versus the rules and guardrails Microsoft has put in place to assure safety. However, even with the strongest of safety provisions, the ultimate arbiter of what aspects of AI's generated outputs, whether they are simple analysis or recommendations on how to proceed forward, is you – the pilot.

Overall, with responsible oversight and accountability, AI data-based insights can be invaluable. But human discretion is essential, especially for choices that significantly impact people. Finding the right balance of AI's exhaustive data processing and human wisdom is key to enhancing business decision making with the help of our new AI-powered copilots.

Action Steps

- What data analysis processes does your business routinely undertake? How could you use AI to make these processes more efficient and accurate?

- Consider the types of decisions your use of AI might influence. Do you have sufficient safeguards around these to ensure qualified human oversight?

10. Leveraging AI for Customer Service and Marketing

Many of the recent high-profile advances in AI involve the abilities of language models to understand human input and generate appropriate original responses. At its core, Microsoft 365 Copilot stands on the shoulders of decades of AI innovation, but really is made possible by this most recent set of forward leaps. It is also these capabilities that open the door to having AI tools that can truly make a useful difference in customer interactions, whether for customer service, for marketing, or other purposes.

It's not that we haven't been trying for some time. How many of us have had the infuriating experience of calling a big company only to be greeted by a robot who is supposed to understand what I'm asking for, but doesn't quite manage it? Or, loading a website, thinking we are chatting with someone in customer service, only to find we are chatting with a bot that can only offer us solutions A-C when we really are looking for solution D?

In the macro sense, tools like Microsoft 365 Copilot are designed to enable our team members to focus less of their time on burdensome paper-pushing, and more on the things that truly make a difference. For many businesses that reallocation of time would naturally mean more capacity to connect with customers, better support of those customers, enhanced service experiences, or more focus on product or service innovation.

However, in a broad sense, AI tooling also offers the capability to directly enhance customer contact, allowing you to elevate every touch point. So, whether you are aiming to deploy a general tool like Microsoft 365 Copilot, or something far more specific, it's likely that the results you are looking for are, either directly or indirectly, connected with enhancing your offering to customers.

Make all communication more productive.

Microsoft's 2023 WorkLab research highlighted the big imbalance many of us feel with always-connected communications tools, with workers spending more than 50% of their time communicating about their work, rather than focusing on the work itself. The feeling of sinking under a sea of emails and chat messages while being unable to escape a constant cycle of meetings is a very real downside of much of our modern technology.

For some time, this has been a focus of various apps and services. Tools like Superhuman or TextExpander seek to alleviate email woes and are even starting to integrate AI capabilities. But with Microsoft 365 Copilot you can push down the accelerator in remediating this problem, by bringing AI abilities to every part of your communications.

Long email thread? No problem, Copilot will summarize it for you. Not sure what to write? No problem, Copilot will give you a first draft, even including relevant content from company documents. Not sure what was agreed during the meeting? No problem, Copilot will give you a breakdown of your actions. Not even able to attend the meeting? No problem, Copilot will give you a report on what happened.

In some ways these capabilities seem the most mundane of the wild things AI tools have started to demonstrate, but alleviating the weight of communications fatigue is perhaps the most impactful way they can help us. The more we can shift the balance to workers focusing on doing rather than emailing back and forth, the more impact we can have on connecting with customers and improving services.

However, streamlining the inboxes of your team members is only one way that AI can enhance your ability to communicate with your customers. Beyond the capabilities of Microsoft 365 Copilot, or the similar tooling to be found in Google Workspace, is a tapestry of tools that can directly and indirectly help you interface with customers quicker, throughout more of the day, and more accurately.

A low-code automation platform like Power Automate can help you connect your Microsoft 365 based messaging, and communications from other services, directly with AI. Using a capability like OpenAI's GPT-3 API (application programing interface), even novices can create workflows that can directly include AI generated outputs, or other aspects of AI tooling such as sentiment analysis. Imagine you receive a serious complaint by email in the middle of the night, using AI powered sentiment analysis and natural language understanding you can ensure that it starts to be dealt with immediately whereas any lower priority issue could wait until the next morning. These types of integrations are now so straightforward that almost anyone could learn how to infuse their flow with AI in an afternoon.

Another part of Microsoft's Power Platform toolset, Power Virtual Agents, allows you to create chatbots that can be deployed through multiple communication channels, including your website. This service has recently undergone an AI focused upgrade that allows users to directly integrate their chatbots with the capabilities of Azure AI Studio. This takes a business' ability to deploy AI with low complexity to a new level by connecting the chatbot experience to your customizations of the underlying AI model. Solutions like this are considerably more complex to deploy than tools like Microsoft 365 Copilot, but the speed at which accessing these sorts of capabilities is becoming simpler is phenomenal. Deeply customized AI based experiences are now well within the reach of even small non-specialist businesses.

All Chatbots Are Not Created Equal

Since the rise of ChatGPT, start-up businesses offering AI-infused chatbot technology seem to have sprung up everywhere. If you haven't already received an offer from someone selling this type of service, you surely soon will!

While these kinds of tools may seem attractive, getting the right technology, and the right skills for implementation is vital. There is a need to tie together customer service, communications, and technical expertise within these systems, which means you need the right people involved on your side of the project.

A chatbot should be designed to make customer service better and more responsive to the customer. It isn't a moat to put around your customer service team to reduce the volume of customer engagement, it should be a mechanism to help them devote their attention to the things that add the most value.

Limited chatbots with no easy route to get to a human can be more frustrating than just waiting longer to begin with. And technology that isn't easy to keep up to date is likely to be a liability when it comes to answering specific questions.

Be careful what you buy in this space, and if it sounds too good to be true, it probably is.

In all cases though, caution does need to be advised with deploying these types of tools, either on an ad-hoc basis on-request through platforms like Microsoft 365 Copilot, or automatically with software like Power Automate, or with purpose-built enterprise solutions.

First, it's important that it is transparent to the recipient of any communication to what extent they are being communicated with by an automated service rather than a human. In the example of Power Virtual Agents, it is recommended that any website or service using automated bot communication flags up that the chat is with a bot at the start of that dialog.

Second, it needs to be clear how and when any AI generated communications will be supervised by a human. It's great that in many cases these tools can now appear more human-like, can generate responses that contain a wider range of more accurate information, and keep a dialog going that better comprehends the needs of the other party – but all these capabilities create bigger risks.

While that big-business phone system that pretends to understand the human voice but ultimately can only do a small number of things might be infuriating, most of its users will work out extremely quickly that it is in fact not a human. This is important as we consider the types of problems such a system might create, where customers might be annoyed to not immediately get a human operator but won't overall be confused or misled by it. An email response generated by GPT-4 can be entirely different, it can appear extremely confident and human-like, but also be totally wrong. Unless the recipient knows that it is AI generated, and what the limitations of that AI tool might be, then you might have customers relying on completely incorrect information if you don't set up the right controls and human supervision in your processes.

You need to address these issues with policy and training as much as with technology. Microsoft is extremely clear as far as anything generated by its Copilot products should be viewed as a first-draft assistant to a human, not a final product to be relied upon. At the very least, the workflow must be to generate the AI supported work, to fully review it for accuracy, and then send; not just to generate and hit send, hoping for the best.

We all play a role in making communication better, and AI can be a valuable tool in that journey. But we must remember that while AI can be a great copilot, it's still necessary for us to lead the way.

Get everyone on board with your brand!

Throughout much of this book, we've focused mostly on the capabilities AI has that help us with work that concerns text and numbers. However, one of the more exciting possibilities that Microsoft 365 Copilot will bring to your office is to also provide support in the visual design of your work.

Over the years the expected degree of sophistication of brand coherence and design from even small businesses has increased dramatically. Gone are the days of clipart and word-art promotional materials, and even basic documents can influence how customers or vendors view the professionalism of a business.

In Microsoft Office, for some time, we have had a robust set of tools to address these needs. We have been able to create templates, and build styles and style libraries, that enable everyone to adopt presentational attributes that align with the branding and stylistic guidelines of their organization. The intent of these tools is that anyone can quickly pull together a document or a PowerPoint presentation and it looks much the same as the similar piece of collateral a coworker created the week before.

However, even with these tools in place, few of us are without colleagues who still find this difficult. You may have people in your office who know their job backwards and forwards but find it impossibly difficult to write an on brand sales proposal or presentation. I know many designers for whom this leads to much hand wringing and more than a few gray hairs.

Luckily, Microsoft 365 Copilot is here to help address this issue, by building the capability to use AI to align the visual design of a document or presentation to an example file in the same way as it's able to use the contents of different files to generate original copy.

Underlying this capability is the fact that modern Office documents are just made up of presentational code, so modifying the layout of a Word document or PowerPoint presentation is technically no more complicated than altering the layout of a website.

Beyond the rearrangement of stylistic elements in documents are other generative capabilities as well. AI tools can generate original images in response to text prompts just as easily as they generate original text responses. While the underlying AI model is a little different, the theory of this is much the same, in that these models are trained on vast troves of images.

OpenAI has a tool called DALL-E which leverages a version of its GPT-3 model to generate images. This is the image generation engine that Microsoft has leveraged in its AI powered tools such as Bing Chat and Microsoft Designer. There are also other, arguably more popular and capable AI image generators available such as Stable Diffusion (for running locally) and Midjourney (running in the cloud).

The field of AI image generation has been beset by its own subset of ethics issues. In substantive ways it is far easier to attribute the influence of model training resulting in a particular image or image style to a certain artist than is the case for generated text. Culturally, we have a nuanced difference in our approach to new work being influenced by text-based work than we do images, and this has led to slightly different discussions around the ethical position of training image generation models than around the connected issues with text.

While it might be entirely practical right now to push a lot of design work from humans to computers using tools like Midjourney, any business considering this should also be aware that there are probably risks in doing so that don't exist, at least not to the same degree, in using AI tools to generate text. Though this is open to change in either direction as legal cases crop up and work their way through courts in various jurisdictions and is something that will be resolved in time.

Taking text and modifying it for your own use is a different process than taking an image and doing the same. It is also far easier to clearly ground text-based responses with your own data, a process that Microsoft 365 Copilot will do organically as you work with it, which means that anything generated will always to a substantial degree be influenced by factors that are unique to your business or situation.

While some forms of use of AI generated imagery may be minimally risky, such as for social media purposes, many businesses may want to pay particular attention to where companies like OpenAI land on image model training data and artist attribution before jumping into those opportunities with both feet.

For many small businesses, who outsource some or all design work, there may be a need to be particularly conscious of how those outside contractors are generating the images you're using. At the very least, you don't want to be paying designer fees for computer generation, but you may also want to ensure that design work is created by a human for now to avoid any attribution risks further down the road.

As with so much connected with AI, there are potentially big upsides to bringing these tools to your business. But it is vital that you fully understand what you are deploying, including the risks, and to mitigate them as far as possible through your policies and procedures. This is a quickly changing issue, like many throughout this book, and you would be well advised to do your own research and seek independent advice.

Action Steps

- Consider what sorts of AI interventions might improve your customer engagement. Do you use specialist systems that need to be integrated with? Do you want to add new channels, like a website chatbot?

- If you outsource design work, review the terms of these engagements around the use of AI work product.

11. AI and Operations: Streamlining Business Processes

Efficiently streamlining operations, whatever those operations are, is imperative to overall productivity, cost efficiency, and value delivery to customers. AI can touch each step of your processes to optimize the flow of work, automate repetition, and bring data-driven intelligence to your supply chains, facilities, or other resources.

Much of this book so far has focused on issues that are most relevant to information workers who spend much of their time at computers or in meetings, but the capabilities of AI can extend into the physical world and impact areas of work such as production lines, warehousing, product delivery, physical security, and many others. However, this is where you step even further outside the capabilities a productivity-focused AI tool like Microsoft 365 Copilot might provide and into the realm of highly specialized tooling or even custom development.

What type of tooling you need entirely depends on the nature of what you do. A web design firm is going to need quite different capabilities from AI than a drink bottling company, but both have options to tool their operations more intelligently. While many team members who are involved in operational processes still receive emails, or attend meetings, or need to review complex documents, so could benefit from the capabilities of a tool like Microsoft 365 Copilot, in these areas the greatest value may come from exploring other options.

The Internet of Things

The Internet of Things or IoT describes a network of interconnected physical devices, vehicles, appliances, and other objects embedded with sensors, software, and connectivity capabilities that enable them to collect vast amounts of data. These devices can range from everyday household objects like smart thermostats and refrigerators to industrial machinery and infrastructure such as manufacturing equipment. IoT technology on its own is not an aspect of AI, but AI techniques like machine learning can be deployed to benefit from the complex data that is associated with various IoT networks.

For example, a machinery manufacturer or servicing business might embed industrial machinery with IoT technology that enables the collection of various metrics about its use or status. This may drive reactive maintenance scheduling by flagging to software when something has broken or is working less than optimally, allowing a service call to be automatically initiated. However, this can be taken to the next level by taking all the data from all the similar machinery that has been deployed, and through using machine learning, creating predictive analytics to optimize the scheduling of proactive maintenance to minimize downtime both from equipment failure and unnecessary routine maintenance.

IoT technology can be deployed increasingly cheaply, and thus is applicable as a tool option in many different scenarios and for smaller businesses than ever before. Additionally, whereas in the past tools to leverage this technology may have required extensive custom development, users of software such as Microsoft Dynamics 365 Field Service can easily integrate IoT data into their maintenance flows, and using Azure IoT Hub and Azure Cognitive Services build customized AI models to predict maintenance needs based on that data. This is certainly significantly more complex than using Microsoft 365 Copilot but is also immensely less complicated than it would have been even a decade ago.

Optimize Scheduling

Whether you are maximizing production in a factory or maximizing seatings in a restaurant, AI capabilities can analyze historical data and see patterns in a way that no human could, to bring efficiency and optimization.

With extensive historical data, AI tools can identify correlations, trends, and seasonal factors that may go unnoticed by human schedulers. By considering variables such as demand patterns, resource availability, and constraints, AI can generate optimized schedules that minimize downtime, reduce bottlenecks, and maximize resource utilization.

In a manufacturing setting, AI-powered scheduling can consider factors such as machine capacity, maintenance requirements, and production targets to generate efficient production schedules. By analyzing historical data on production volumes, equipment performance, and maintenance records, AI can identify optimal production sequences and minimize changeovers, resulting in increased throughput and reduced costs. Tools like Microsoft Dynamics 365 Supply Chain Management can open the door to easily deploying these types of technology capabilities, but there are a wide range of tools available for very specific use cases.

Similarly, in a restaurant or hospitality setting, AI can leverage historical data on customer demand, reservation patterns, and table turnover rates to optimize seating arrangements and reservation schedules. By considering factors like customer preferences, party sizes, and seating capacity, AI algorithms can generate optimal seating plans, reducing waiting times, maximizing occupancy, and enhancing overall customer satisfaction. Platforms like OpenTable help restaurants to efficiently maximize the value of their space while also offering customers an easy and accessible way to automate their interactions with the business. As we now see AI options enter this market, such tools will become even more efficient in satisfying the needs of each customer while maximizing revenue.

Computer vision is beginning to become important to these sorts of scenarios. In that restaurant, there may often be a disparity between what the reservation system tells us, what the point-of-sale system tells us, and what is the reality of the space usage on a particular day. Using AI powered vision systems, it is now possible to not just rely on disconnected data repositories, but for your tools to truly "see" what is going on, how long parties really stay, how much time it takes for tables to be cleared, and who is the most productive server. These are fascinating, but potentially intrusive tools, and businesses must strike a balance between the operating benefits of such capabilities versus the privacy of customers and employees.

Through techniques like these AI can also help to improve and rebalance the experience of work of frontline or manual workers. Poor scheduling can lead to an overwhelming or even unsafe production environment, and imbalances in opportunities like overtime. In hospitality, a shift where servers are run off their feet and unable to provide a good customer experience followed by a slow shift with few customers both hurt the team members by reducing customer tips and the business. Adding AI tooling to scheduling is not only important to business efficiency and productivity, but also to create an engaged, low-turnover staff team too.

Optimize Space

Similarly, to optimized scheduling, AI offers opportunities to improve how you utilize and maintain space, whether considering the utilization of meeting rooms in an office or of warehouse capacity connected to a delivery dock.

Such optimizations can rely upon other technology such as that covered when looking at IoT above. For example, smart thermostats connected with meeting scheduling data and human presence detection can allow you to optimize the use of

HVAC in your buildings reducing fuel costs and maintenance needs. Coupled with AI such capabilities can move from reactive to predictive, taking data you can already gather and act upon, and using it to draw new conclusions that help you optimize further.

One of the first practical experiences I had of using AI was in the academic timetabling world. Here, complex tools could analyze vast amounts of data coming from massive groups of students, complex buildings spread across vast areas, and class data, and come up with various predictions to help understand how space might be used. At this point the AI did little, and human supervisors did a lot, but such tools have now advanced and are many times more capable.

The possibilities to leverage AI outside of the intangible world of emails and chat messages, and into our real-world facilities, and tangible tools and equipment, are endless. The new AI capabilities that are advancing around us put into the hands of anyone the ability to bring more intelligence to whatever it is you do, whether on a computer screen or elsewhere. Tools like Microsoft 365 Copilot address only some of these needs, and in the same way that Microsoft PowerPoint has never been that useful to welders, will not be the most appropriate surfacing of AI capabilities for everyone. But there is certainly a reason for everyone to be excited about the potential of this technology, even if they don't do their job sitting at a desk!

As we think about our copilot, we also need to think about the vehicle we are piloting. The direction may be set from the cockpit, but it's the engines, wheels, and other parts of the mechanical system that get us where we are going. Our AI journey may start within arm's length of where we are sitting, but we should have our eyes open to long-term possibilities where there are new tools that can touch every part of what we do to great benefit.

12. AI Risk Management: Mitigating Potential Pitfalls

AI offers amazing potential, but it also comes with risks that demand prudent management and constant monitoring. Like any transformative technology, there will be bumps in the road toward maturity, and issues of improper implementation or oversight will lead to some unintended consequences. These could include opaque decision-making, or built-in biases, and as we've learned from previous chapters, these are not theoretical concerns but ones that have already emerged.

Throughout this book we have mostly framed risk through the lens of ethics, and while this is incredibly important, there are other areas where we should be conscious that AI tools may not be a panacea in addressing already present or new problems. Your approach to monitoring risk, updating your list of potential risks, and evaluating performance to see whether risks have been realized is vital across several areas.

Unrealistic Expectations

The excitement that currently abounds around AI is contagious, and whether you are truly passionate about this technology or just wanting to get on board in case you miss some opportunity down the road, you clearly have caught the bug. But, while it is certainly exciting, it isn't the answer to every problem, and isn't even the answer to most problems.

In chapter 4, we mapped out steps you can take around evaluating AI performance to understand the pace of change and measure incremental progress. It is important to set realistic goals and timelines for AI adoption, rather than expecting overnight transformations. AI involves gradual integration and learning. Leaders must temper expectations, set incremental goals, and allow time for humans and AI systems to perfect new capabilities.

In chapter 3, we considered having expectations around AI that are grounded in the technology as it currently exists, rather than ideas around where it may develop that are currently, and for some time, fiction. Even the most cutting-edge AI tools fail to impress when they are viewed solely through this type of lens.

Now, and for some years to come, your most important tools for the success of your business will be your knowledge and that of your experienced team members. Don't be impatient for AI, take the proven benefits as they come, be open to exploration, and create a culture where tools like these can be embraced. Don't set unrealistic targets, timelines, or expectations.

Technical Debt

When we refer to "technical debt" we are considering burdens that accumulate in our technology that makes things difficult to support or manage. Issues such as integration workarounds, poorly organized data, out-of-date infrastructure, or quick-fixes layered one-on-top of the other, fall into this category. This can be a real problem with any technology, but particularly when trying to deal with something new that is rapidly changing.

Starting out with AI, the most concerning technical debt issue may well be its access to your data. If you have poor governance practices, oversharing or under sharing, or you're relying on a patchwork of barely connected systems, then any AI implementation that seeks to benefit from data from across your organization will be an uphill struggle.

But the early implementation of AI tools itself may also cause problems. Not so much with licensed commercial products like

Microsoft 365 Copilot, but with low-code solutions you might try out, or custom development based on one of the AI providers' API capabilities. "Move fast and break things", may be a famous mantra that has served at least some of the big tech companies well, but it's not an approach recommended for most businesses.

Culture Gaps

In chapters 4 and 7 we dug deeply into various aspects of preparing your team for changes driven by AI. No matter how successful you are in this endeavor, the nature of the types of impact AI might have should mean maintaining a positive culture around it is something you pay close and ongoing attention to.

Through the next chapter you will learn some of what Microsoft has stated as its plans for how AI will change how we use technology. You can use your own judgement for your own business as to whether through that development the impetus is likely to stay on augmenting human employees rather than seriously altering or eliminating what they do day-to-day.

Attitudes toward AI and the culture around it in your business may not be totally under your control. External factors may influence your AI journey and you cannot assume that because you engaged everyone up front that engagement perpetuates endlessly and positively.

Costs

For companies like OpenAI who are at the bleeding edge of AI innovation, the costs associated with their product development and maintenance are eye watering. A single processing card needed to train and refine AI models can cost in the five-figures, and these are not resources used only by the handful. It is not yet guaranteed that models like GPT-4 can continue to improve while being offered cheaply to users for a seemingly endless list of potential tasks.

Additionally, training these models has relied upon a flow of data from the Internet which has been accessible for free. But publishers of websites that may have content that has been used for model training are quickly catching onto this and making assertions of their right to be financially compensated for the data being used, or just shutting down the flow of data entirely.

There is an endless slew of factors that indicate that AI's cheap and unregulated initial boom might get bogged down in costs, regulation, and litigation, that either reduces the efficacy of these tools, limits access, or just makes them far more expensive than they are now.

In various markets, like transportation or food delivery, we have experienced the tech start-up approach of disrupt an industry with loss-leading cheap prices, and then when consumers are hooked and incumbents are eliminated or weakened, skyrocket the price. Flipped the other way but with the same impact are changes like the move from on-premises perpetual software licensing to cloud-based software monthly fees, which has allowed companies like Adobe or Microsoft to turn already profitable operations into money-printing machines.

Once you have retooled for AI, how much would AI need to start costing you to go back the other way? Would someone who's got used to summarized email threads rather than sitting up late at night reading individual messages be concerned about a 2x increase? How about a 5x? How about a 10x?

There is a risk here that should not be overblown but also should not be underestimated. Notwithstanding the hiring difficulties of the post-pandemic period, our spend on technology has increased more rapidly than the average wages of employees in the sort of job roles where AI's talents currently have most impact. There are lots of good and beneficial reasons to adopt AI that can enhance our businesses and our employees' lives, but we cannot be 100% certain in the long-term that the overall cost to our businesses will be balanced by ongoing increases in revenue or production. This all depends on AI continuing to get better while also remaining relatively cheap.

Societal Impacts

What if widely deployed AI systems start to make a lot of bad decisions? What if entry-level employees start to struggle to get or keep jobs because of the impact of AI? What if AI is responsible for election interference or misinformation?

There are many unintended impacts that could arise from this current development of AI that could make its use frowned upon or raise a diverse set of ethical considerations for business owners who were continuing to deploy it. This is a genie that will never get back into its bottle, but changes in customer attitudes, and changes in regulation, could make it far harder to use AI at the small business scale without significant additional compliance overhead.

For each person who thinks these sorts of concerns are nonsense, there's another who thinks we are playing with fire by engaging at all with this new AI. This is exactly why we track risks; these are not things guaranteed to happen, nor even likely to happen, but regardless of this we should be aware of them as possibilities to be able to protect our businesses, our teams, and the communities.

Does this mean we should look with suspicion as we glance over at the copilot's seat? Not if you have done your due diligence up until now. If you have engaged with your team and customers well, if you have mitigated the ethical concerns around your use of AI, and if you have tracked risks in a suitable way, you should be well placed to ride out a little rain, or some stormy skies.

13. Microsoft's Copiloted Future

As I start writing this chapter, I've just finished some sessions on the first day of Microsoft's 2023 Inspire partner conference. In just a few short months, the Copilot brand has gone from being a niche product for coders who use GitHub, to something that is more present in Microsoft's product stack than either Office or Windows. At one of the sessions, a Microsoft employee noted that neither AI nor Copilot had been mentioned yet about 15-minutes in and joked that she needed to start talking about it to hit quota. While I'm sure there isn't really a quota to be filled, this sudden Copilot everywhere approach does not just come organically from the natural AI-evolution of each of the associated products.

When Microsoft 365 Copilot was announced in March 2023, I released a YouTube video entitled "Microsoft Just Won Work!". It was the kind of technology that upon seeing it welled excitement in a way that a trailer for an upcoming movie blockbuster might rather than a demo of a piece of business software. As time has gone on and that announcement has proliferated into Copilots everywhere, the initial excitement has not dissipated, but questions about what this means to someone who chooses to use Microsoft's software stack have grown.

Having many Copilots does not seem to be the streamlined sci-fi future that was initially imagined. In Star Trek, when Captain Picard makes a request starting with the word "Computer", I don't remember him ever having to make sure he was standing next to the right computer terminal for the type of request he was making; and frankly, I didn't imagine we would have to be working in the right Copilot to get whatever it is we wanted to get done completed. The breakdown of Microsoft's Copilot products shown in chapter 3, goes some way to them starting to unpick this knot, but even with a three-tiered approach to an overarching "Microsoft Copilot" there are still capabilities that invariably seem to fall to *different* copilots.

Hopefully, this is a technical limitation, but I fear more likely it is a licensing one. Rather than Copilot being a pervasive concept through Microsoft's software, having it in Word might be a different license than having it in SharePoint or having it connected to your security administration experience, and each of these tools will come with their own small monthly increase to your Microsoft invoice. We know the price of Microsoft 365 Copilot, but whether other AI capabilities will continue to exist in the scope of existing licenses or inside new ones in the long-term is unknown.

At Microsoft's Build conference a few weeks before Inspire, the second day keynote had an illuminating talk given by Steve Bathiche, a Microsoft Technical Fellow. He broke down the path of AI as a three-step approach with three different application structures.

"In the first application structure, the AI is beside your application, helping. Helping your tasks. Being a helper. It's like a copilot. It is a copilot. It's very appropriate that the first types of significant experiences are copilots because it enables us to get in the game quickly. It keeps the original app architecture definition and is [not] mentally disruptive to what our customers already know."

This is where we are now at, with Copilot side panels popping up in our applications but with the original application and the same input capabilities still there for us to use.

"In the second application structure the AI is inside as the main scaffolding of the app. It's the main input loop. Here, you use AI to completely redefine the application interaction model and even its purpose. The interaction model will be less dependent on point-and-click commands. Things will become much more automatic. [...] Here there are fewer toolbars, fewer deep menus, simply because you don't need them. You want to just intuitively direct the app with what you're managing, and this task is accomplished within the context of the application."

So, we can expect that the 2.0 versions of these initial Copilot offerings move from side panels to deeper integrations, where at least some of the complexity of the UI vanishes into a set of tasks that are more organically supported by the AI.

"And this brings us to the third and final application structure, where AI goes from executing from within the context of the application frame to AI being outside, executing globally. Here, [...] I orchestrate across multiple apps, plugins and services, functioning more as an agent."

With the goal being that your interface to all you are doing is the AI and it guides your tasks across the different capabilities of the software and platforms you have access to without you needing to worry specifically about individual software actions.

This seems utopian but also contrary to the way Microsoft has established its Copilot product stack and licensing. The announced per user monthly add-on fee for Microsoft 365 Copilot is just for that individual Copilot and other Copilots, such as Sales Copilot in Dynamics 365, come with additional fees or as part of separate licenses.

In Steve's talk he also showed a video highlighting that it has now been 50 years since the original demonstration of a keyboard and mouse as computer input devices. These were later popularized by the Mac and Windows and continue to be our main interface into our computing devices today.

However, imagine if back in the 1970s, Steve Jobs and Bill Gates had looked at the mouse and conceived it as an application specific tool, one where you needed a mouse with a certain button configuration to use a word processor, and another for a spreadsheet. And further imagine that instead of a mouse being a static piece of equipment, it was something that got updated regularly, and Apple or Microsoft charged you a monthly fee for this service, month-after-month, for as long as you needed the tools it worked with.

If these copilots will evolve to be the new mouse and keyboard then under the SaaS (software-as-a-service) licensing model that is ubiquitous today, Microsoft has started us on a very different journey with this interface technology than the one that saw a mouse and keyboard thrown into every PC shipping box from the 1980s through to today.

Will we reach a point where the AI powered interface is so easily integrated and ubiquitous that it will just be thrown in with any new software? Or will Microsoft be hesitant to give up some of its recurring income gained through the development of Copilot, and so act as a gatekeeper of what can and cannot be done with a computer in a vastly different way than we see today? Any students of the history of capitalism should know and be concerned by the likely answer.

These are undoubtedly exceedingly important and exciting technologies that have the potential to revolutionize work in ways outlined throughout the previous chapters. Microsoft has conceived a vision for AI, connected with its dominant position in the business productivity market to map out a different reality of what work might look like in years to come. But, alongside this it has also mapped out benefits that transcend business outcomes to changing the lives of workers in terms of stress, balance, access, and equity.

It is easy to see how Microsoft can deliver on the promise of transforming work. But to transform people's lives inside and outside of work requires a different approach, an approach where the technology is a democratizing and leveling force, and one where the benefits are shared.

Microsoft has talked the good talk on these societal considerations with its AI development. However, the proliferation of Copilots, and the associated proliferation of different license tiers and costs, shows the first signs of cracks where these utopian ideals hit the reality of Microsoft being one of the world's largest commercial entities.

When Microsoft Windows arrived in 1985, few foresaw the direction that the computing age would take us over the next 40 years. We are now significantly more aware as a society of the power big technology changes in this field have to alter our life experience, and this means companies like Microsoft are under far more pressure to account for the good their products will do from the outset.

14. The growing AI arms race: Introducing Bard, Claude, and a cast of thousands.

Highlighted throughout the previous chapters are examples of AI capabilities surfaced by companies other than Microsoft and even ones dating back decades that have mapped out the path of where we currently find ourselves today.

The revolutionary AI capabilities delivered by a large language model (LLM) like OpenAI's GPT-4 are amazing but not unique. There are other companies in the LLM space, and ones with models that can compete in some areas with OpenAI's technology.

A company like Anthropic has developed Claude and Claude 2 which delivers capabilities extremely like that of ChatGPT. At the time of writing Claude 2 is in beta but offers great promise in relation to its overall abilities versus GPT-4.

Whereas you may not have heard of Anthropic, you most likely have heard of Meta, and they have jumped into the AI space too. They have focused on developing open-source large language models called Llama, and some of these are small enough to be able to be used locally on a PC easily.

Alongside these developments, AI is popping up everywhere. If you use a website builder like Squarespace, you'll see you can now use generative AI to build content. If you use an HR tool like Teamflect, you'll see that you can summarize employee feedback with AI.

While all these models or features are somewhat interesting, in an analysis of Microsoft 365 Copilot, and Microsoft's wider Copilot platform, the only other company that is currently worth looking at is Google.

That's not because Microsoft or Google's AI tech is currently more sophisticated than competitors, though in the case of OpenAI's GPT-4 which Microsoft is using that could be argued, but because they are the only companies capable of teaming AI with day-to-day productivity and mountains of your business' existing data.

They both have a perfect trifecta of tooling to revolutionize how AI is used in your day-to-day work lives. They have access to powerful AI models. They have the tools, in Microsoft Office, or Google Workspace, where you spend time doing work. And they have the data that gives context to your work; your emails, your company's price lists, your logos, and your various policies and procedures.

Ultimately, the AI tool most suitable for your business needs will be down to what you are trying to achieve. This book has mainly focused on the copilot type of technology that acts as a generalized productivity assistant in whatever you would normally be doing day-to-day. But this development hasn't only brought about new tools like Microsoft 365 Copilot, but also made it easier for anyone to access the underlying models that are powering these technologies.

Through using the OpenAI API (application programing interface) for example coupled with low-code app or automation building tools like Microsoft Power Platform, practically anyone could build a tool that uses AI capabilities in a few hours or less. This is an entirely revolutionary workflow and opens the doors to many opportunities both directly and indirectly tied to the AI space for businesses of any size.

It seems unlikely that in the foreseeable future any company will be able to usurp the market dominance Microsoft and Google have in business productivity and therefore their AI tools will become the most ubiquitous. There is an outside chance Amazon could do something here, or perhaps Apple will focus on its tooling like Pages or Keynote in an entirely unexpected way, but the likelihood some unknown start-up will shift aside Microsoft Office should probably be seen as low to none.

While the generalized, inside or next to your productivity tool AI capabilities like Microsoft 365 Copilot might be the most accessible, they are probably not the most interesting. In the background will be the fight for AI inside more specialized tools like video editing software, desktop publishing, web design, data analytics, and even areas where we cross from IT to OT (operational technology) that is the brains for major industry and national infrastructure.

Also exciting is the potential for non-technology businesses to amplify their own thinking processes with others through deploying AI. If you are a leader in your field at doing anything, and you have gotten there through your own proprietary approach to using the data around you, you can potentially now train an AI model to think in a comparable way and monetize that. Say you're a realtor with a successful approach to identifying potential sale opportunities based on a unique process for analyzing historic sale trends. Not only can you scale up that approach by using AI for your own business, but potentially you can scale out that approach by building apps with AI tools trained on that thinking which you can then sell or license to competitors. Whereas in the past the only reasonable route to amplify that knowledge in a separate way may have been to engage in business training seminars, now, instead of teaching others how to think like you, you can simply sell them a tool that thinks for them.

The last area to consider is how AI might change how we collect and share data. With the release of Bing Chat, Microsoft changed web search by making it a dialog, and pulling information from the web into their chats rather than sending users to specific websites (users are still linked to websites, but it's not necessary to go there if the chat has already answered the question).

Google quickly followed up on this by releasing its own equivalent product called Bard, and ChatGPT even added a capability to crawl the web with Bing for its ChatGPT Plus subscribers. Tools like these mean that users are sharing information very differently to how they have been for decades using products like Google search, and getting used to the principle of finding what they need through dialog rather than sequential searches.

This radically shakes up how users access information but also what information they share to gain that access. For publishers online this creates risks (what happens if no one clicks on the links that are surfaced), but for websites that can gain traffic, also opportunities to alter how the relationship with the end-user is built. This new world of online search and where web traffic ends up may ultimately be more impactful for companies like Google and Microsoft (note that Google generates a phenomenal amount of its revenue from online advertising), than the AI tools they are selling to their business customers. For small businesses, keeping an eye on search and advertising trends is more important than ever as if your main storefront for the world to see is your website, we may not know how that experience will change, but we can know that AI will change it.

Conclusion: Embracing AI as Your Business Copilot

After a journey covering a dizzying variety of AI and AI-connected topics as they may apply to any small business, we are nearing our destination, and we need to land. You look over at the copilot's seat and you have a decision to make. Is this new colleague or partner to be trusted to get you safely back to the runway, or do you need to grab the controls?

How your business works with AI is a decision that only you and your team can make. Each situation will be different, with different processes, different technical debt, and a different level of willingness to embrace and learn about technology. Even your perception of the ethics of using AI in business or the impact it may be having on our society will be unique to you, and to the customers you work with day-to-day.

Whatever your approach to AI, having a good understanding of what it is, its capabilities, and its direction of travel will be important in the coming months and years. This isn't just technology that **might** revolutionize how we work, it already is. Whether it's for the business next door or a competitor several states over, or the marketing company you just hired for a campaign, AI is out there and it's having an impact.

Adopting a tool like Microsoft 365 Copilot may be the first step in your AI journey, but over time it probably won't be the last. As these technologies mature their utility in lots of situations will increase and for certain functions at least, the argument for human augmentation rather than human replacement will change. Your earlier work to create a solid foundation for the role of AI in your business will empower you when that time comes as you will have invested effort in building the capabilities of your team, creating familiarity with change, and having a long-term proactive approach to maximizing with AI rather than reacting to it.

This will be a generational shift in how work is done and an opportunity to reinforce those good things that have come from the dawn of the computer-age through the Internet-age, but also an opportunity to change direction on those things that are problematic. It is easy to imagine a future where AI leads to mass job elimination, where human workers are mainly involved in manual work that computers still lack robotic technology to complete. But it is just as easy to imagine a future where AI creates more balance for humans, where we can focus more time on things that are for the good of all while not sacrificing productivity, and where we can promote equity, fairness, and mental- and physical-wellbeing. Ultimately, you are the pilot, you will define the direction of travel, and while your journey may only be one of many, each will mark a small step along the path of where this relationship between human-intelligence and artificial-intelligence will, finally, land.

In our journey, we just landed. It's time to turn off the fasten seatbelts sign and disembark. The next step in this path is up to you. Equipped with new knowledge on AI and approaches to implementing it, I'm sure you will choose it wisely, and you will treat your copilot well.

How was AI used in writing this book?

Writing a book about the advent of AI as a tool for all our work processes and then ignoring its capabilities in that work would be both ironic and a missed opportunity to demonstrate the transformative potential of the technology in action.

In keeping with the capabilities of the technology and usage best practices, AI was used to help to broadly structure and draft the outline of the book, to assist in research, and to improve the clarity of some sections. The content is human-written and AI-assisted, as any content generated using AI now and for some time, should be.

The AI tool used for this was mainly ChatGPT, and specifically ChatGPT using the GPT-4 model with the Bing web access capabilities turned on (until this feature disappeared late in the writing process – a cautionary tale for relying too much on nascent tools!). For some sections, research was conducted using the Bing Chat capability, mainly with the "Precise" response option turned on. And later, some review was also done in the Claude 2 beta.

For its part, this is how ChatGPT described its work on this book when I prompted:

Nick: Based on this chat so far, and what you've seen of the final parts of my writing I have shared with you, write a short 100-word section titled "How was AI used in the writing of this book?".

ChatGPT: In crafting this book, we've leveraged AI—specifically, advanced language models like ChatGPT. These tools have assisted with everything from topic research to drafting content. They've provided real-time fact-checking, surfaced relevant academic studies, and suggested phrasing improvements. By illustrating AI's role in the creation of this very book, we underscore its transformative potential across diverse applications.

Nick: Do you think you should be attributed as the author of our work?

ChatGPT: As an artificial intelligence, I don't have consciousness, beliefs, or desires, so I don't require or seek any form of attribution or authorship. My purpose is to assist and facilitate, rather than to create original works in my own right. Therefore, any attribution should go to the human authors who designed the research questions, made key decisions, and interpreted and edited the text that I helped to generate.

Nick: Is there anything you would like to add that should be included in this section to help readers understand your work assisting on a project like this?

ChatGPT: To fully understand the role of AI in a project like this, it's important to note that while AI can generate comprehensive responses, it doesn't have understanding, beliefs, or creativity in the human sense. AI operates based on patterns, rules, and data provided to it, making it a tool rather than a collaborator. It can help expedite the writing process and handle repetitive tasks, but it ultimately relies on human guidance and input. The value of AI lies in its ability to provide information quickly, sift through large amounts of data, and provide suggestions based on patterns it has learned. But the final interpretation, analysis, and presentation of information are solely human endeavors.

Ultimately, it is important to understand that AI can augment, support, and make your process easier, but it is not the creative driver of your work. For whatever you do, I hope you will choose to try to use AI to make it better, but to do so in a way that is understanding of the technology's limitations and presents its work with transparency in mind.

Further Reading

This section highlights many of the sources that were used in the writing of this book, along with other useful resources you might seek out to expand your understanding of specific topics.

1. AI and You: The New Business Landscape

- Scrutinizing the effects of digital technology on mental health, Nature, Jonathan Haidt & Nick Allen, 2020 - https://www.nature.com/articles/d41586-020-00296-x
- History of A.I.: Artificial Intelligence (Infographic), Karl Tate, 2014 - https://www.livescience.com/47544-history-of-a-i-artificial-intelligence-infographic.html
- Microsoft outlines framework for building AI apps and copilots; expands AI plugin ecosystem, Microsoft, John Roach, 2023 - https://news.microsoft.com/source/features/ai/microsoft-outlines-framework-for-building-ai-apps-and-copilots-expands-ai-plugin-ecosystem/

2. Understanding AI: Basics for Business Leaders

- What is generative AI?, McKinsey & Company, 2023 - https://www.mckinsey.com/featured-insights/mckinsey-explainers/what-is-generative-ai
- What is Explainable AI?, IBM - https://www.ibm.com/watson/explainable-ai
- The Problem With Biased AIs (and How To Make AI Better), Forbes, Barnard Marr, 2022 - https://www.forbes.com/sites/bernardmarr/2022/09/30

/the-problem-with-biased-ais-and-how-to-make-ai-better/
- Companies That Replace People with AI Will Get Left Behind, Harvard Business Review, Behnam Tabrizi and Babak Pahlavan, 2023 - https://hbr.org/2023/06/companies-that-replace-people-with-ai-will-get-left-behind

3. The Productivity Benefits of a Copilot

- Number of companies using Office 365 worldwide as of February 2023, by leading country, Statista, 2023 - https://www.statista.com/statistics/983321/worldwide-office-365-user-numbers-by-country/
- Microsoft acquires Nuance—makers of Dragon speech rec—for $16 billion, ArsTechnica, Jim Salter, 2021 - https://arstechnica.com/gadgets/2021/04/microsoft-acquires-nuance-makers-of-dragon-speech-rec-for-16-billion/
- AI has a long way to go before doctors can trust it with your life, Quartz, Gary Smith and Jeffrey Funk, 2021 - https://qz.com/2016153/ai-promised-to-revolutionize-radiology-but-so-far-its-failing
- Microsoft finalizes its acquisition of Nuance Communications, ZDNet, Mary Jo Foley, 2022 - https://www.zdnet.com/article/microsoft-finalizes-its-acquisition-of-nuance-communications/
- A Complete Guide to Natural Language Processing, DeepLearning.AI, 2023 - https://www.deeplearning.ai/resources/natural-language-processing/

4. Strategic Considerations for AI in Business

- Microsoft Teams usage jumps 50 percent to 115 million daily active users, The Verge, Tom Warren, 2020 - https://www.theverge.com/2020/10/27/21537286/microsoft-teams-115-million-daily-active-users-stats

- Microsoft Assessments, Microsoft - https://learn.microsoft.com/en-us/assessments/
- How Americans think about artificial intelligence, Pew Research Center, Lee Rainie, Cary Funk, Monica Anderson and Alec Tyson, 2022 - https://www.pewresearch.org/internet/2022/03/17/how-americans-think-about-artificial-intelligence/

5. Leadership in the Age of AI: Guiding Your Team Forward

- How COVID-19 has pushed companies over the technology tipping point—and transformed business forever, McKinsey & Company, 2020 - https://www.mckinsey.com/capabilities/strategy-and-corporate-finance/our-insights/how-covid-19-has-pushed-companies-over-the-technology-tipping-point-and-transformed-business-forever
- Microsoft 365 Copilot Adoption, Microsoft - https://adoption.microsoft.com/en-us/copilot/

6. Planning Tools and Approaches: Understanding and Analyzing Your Processes

- Overview of Microsoft Graph, Microsoft, 2023 - https://learn.microsoft.com/en-us/graph/overview
- Empowering every developer with plugins for Microsoft 365 Copilot, Microsoft, Rajesh Jha, 2023 - https://www.microsoft.com/en-us/microsoft-365/blog/2023/05/23/empowering-every-developer-with-plugins-for-microsoft-365-copilot/
- What is shadow IT?, Cloudflare - https://www.cloudflare.com/learning/access-management/what-is-shadow-it
- Microsoft launches Power Automate Process Mining and next-generation AI, Microsoft, Justin Graham, 2023 - https://cloudblogs.microsoft.com/powerplatform/2023/

07/18/microsoft-launches-power-automate-process-mining-and-next-generation-ai/

7. Preparing Your Workforce: HR Strategies for the AI Era

- Are AI Recruitment Tools Ethical And Efficient? The Pros And Cons Of ATS, Forbes, Kara Dennison, 2022 - https://www.forbes.com/sites/karadennison/2022/06/27/are-ai-recruitment-tools-ethical-and-efficient-the-pros-and-cons-of-ats
- OpenAI discontinues its AI writing detector due to "low rate of accuracy", ArsTechnica, Benj Edwards, 2023 - https://arstechnica.com/information-technology/2023/07/openai-discontinues-its-ai-writing-detector-due-to-low-rate-of-accuracy/
- Introducing Microsoft 365 Copilot—A whole new way to work, Microsoft, Colette Stallbaumer, 2023 - https://www.microsoft.com/en-us/microsoft-365/blog/2023/03/16/introducing-microsoft-365-copilot-a-whole-new-way-to-work
- Samsung workers made a major error by using ChatGPT, TechRadar, Lewis Maddison, 2023 - https://www.techradar.com/news/samsung-workers-leaked-company-secrets-by-using-chatgpt
- Bing Chat Enterprise, Microsoft, 2023 - https://www.microsoft.com/en-us/edge/bing/chat-enterprise
- How white engineers built racist code – and why it's dangerous for black people, The Guardian, Ali Breland, 2017 - https://www.theguardian.com/technology/2017/dec/04/racist-facial-recognition-white-coders-black-people-police

8. AI and Privacy: Navigating Legal and Ethical Considerations

- Why the biggest challenge facing AI is an ethical one, BBC, Bryan Lufkin, 2017 - https://www.bbc.com/future/article/20170307-the-ethical-challenge-facing-artificial-intelligence
- Universal Declaration of Human Rights, Amnesty International - https://www.amnesty.org/en/what-we-do/universal-declaration-of-human-rights/
- Complete guide to GDPR compliance - https://gdpr.eu/
- Privacy and responsible AI, iapp, Katharina Koerner, 2022 - https://iapp.org/news/a/privacy-and-responsible-ai/
- Empowering responsible AI practices, Microsoft - https://www.microsoft.com/en-us/ai/responsible-ai
- Recommendation on the Ethics of Artificial Intelligence, UNESCO, 2022 - https://unesdoc.unesco.org/ark:/48223/pf0000381137
- Ethics of Artificial Intelligence, UNESCO - https://www.unesco.org/en/artificial-intelligence/recommendation-ethics
- Amazon scraps secret AI recruiting tool that showed bias against women, Jeffrey Dastin, 2018 - https://www.reuters.com/article/us-amazon-com-jobs-automation-insight-idUSKCN1MK08G

9. The Role of AI in Decision-Making and Analysis

- The Impact Of Artificial Intelligence On Leadership: How To Leverage AI To Improve Decision-Making, Forbes, Kara Dennison, 2023 - https://www.forbes.com/sites/karadennison/2023/03/14/the-impact-of-artificial-intelligence-on-leadership-how-to-leverage-ai-to-improve-decision-making/
- Ethical Issues in Advanced Artificial Intelligence, Nick Bostrom, 2003 - https://nickbostrom.com/ethics/ai

- What is the AI alignment problem and how can it be solved?, New Scientist, Edd Gent, 2023 - https://www.newscientist.com/article/mg25834382-000-what-is-the-ai-alignment-problem-and-how-can-it-be-solved/

10. Leveraging AI for Customer Service and Marketing

- Will AI Fix Work?, Microsoft WorkLab, 2023 - https://www.microsoft.com/en-us/worklab/work-trend-index/will-ai-fix-work
- Create Generative AI solutions with Power Virtual Agents and Azure OpenAI Services, Microsoft, Sarah Critchley, 2023 - https://powervirtualagents.microsoft.com/en-us/blog/create-generative-ai-solutions-with-power-virtual-agents-and-azure-openai-services/
- DALL·E 2, OpenAI - https://openai.com/dall-e-2
- High-Resolution Image Synthesis with Latent Diffusion Models, Stable Diffusion, Robin Rombach et al. - https://ommer-lab.com/research/latent-diffusion-models/
- Generative AI Has an Intellectual Property Problem, Harvard Business Review, Gil Appel, Juliana Neelbauer, and David A. Schweidel, 2023 - https://hbr.org/2023/04/generative-ai-has-an-intellectual-property-problem

11. AI and Operations: Streamlining Business Processes

- What is IoT?, Microsoft - https://azure.microsoft.com/en-us/resources/cloud-computing-dictionary/what-is-iot
- Using AI in predictive maintenance to forecast the future, Deloitte - https://www2.deloitte.com/us/en/pages/consulting/articles/using-ai-in-predictive-maintenance.html

- Computer Vision For The Restaurant Industry (2023 Guide), Viso.ai, Gaudenz Boesch, 2023 - https://viso.ai/applications/restaurant/

12. AI Risk Management: Mitigating Potential Pitfalls

- Measuring And Managing Technical Debt, Forbes, Ken Knapton, 2022 - https://www.forbes.com/sites/forbestechcouncil/2022/08/10/measuring-and-managing-technical-debt
- Reddit will begin charging for access to its API, TechCrunch, Kyle Wiggers, 2023 - https://techcrunch.com/2023/04/18/reddit-will-begin-charging-for-access-to-its-api/
- Gartner Says More Than Half of Enterprise IT Spending in Key Market Segments Will Shift to the Cloud by 2025, Gartner, 2022 - https://www.gartner.com/en/newsroom/press-releases/2022-02-09-gartner-says-more-than-half-of-enterprise-it-spending

13. Microsoft's Copiloted Future

- Introducing Microsoft 365 Copilot—A whole new way to work, Microsoft, Colette Stallbaumer, 2023 - https://www.microsoft.com/en-us/microsoft-365/blog/2023/03/16/introducing-microsoft-365-copilot-a-whole-new-way-to-work/
- Microsoft Just Won Work!, Bright Ideas Agency, Nick DeCourcy, 2023 - https://youtu.be/C11p_-w-g8c
- Shaping the future of work with AI, Microsoft, 2023 - https://build.microsoft.com/en-US/sessions/8aab36d1-d27d-46dd-81ec-eb3f49cfee6a

14. The Growing AI Arms Race: Introducing Bard, Claude, and a Cast of Thousands

- An important next step on our AI journey, Google, Sundar Pichai, 2023 – https://blog.google/technology/ai/bard-google-ai-search-updates/
- Introducing Claude, Anthropic, 2023 – https://www.anthropic.com/index/introducing-claude
- Meta AI's Llama 2, Meta, 2023 - https://ai.meta.com/llama/

About the author

Nick DeCourcy has been a lifelong technology enthusiast dreaming of the autonomous computer systems seen in utopian science fiction movies. Now, as owner and principal consultant at Bright Ideas Agency, he helps small business leaders take the steps that will help them thrive in this new AI-enabled era.

Nick specializes in Microsoft 365 and Power Platform. He advises businesses on a range of issues including technology adoption, digital transformation, and productization of IP.

Prior to this, he spent 20 years working in various operations leadership roles across several industries. He has seen the impact good technology can have on effective operations, and customer and team experience. He has also experienced poorly planned technology change, and learned from the negative impact it can have on effectiveness and morale.

Nick is originally from London, England, but currently resides in Cincinnati, Ohio. As well as his consulting work, he is a technology YouTuber and blogger, and is active in several Microsoft 365 focused online communities. When not doing technology, he is a husband and a dad, as well as a dog and chicken owner. He also enjoys home renovation projects and is currently working on his 120-year-old house.

LinkedIn: https://linkedin.com/in/nickdc/

YouTube: https://youtube.com/@brightideasagency

Website: https://brightideasagency.com

Printed in Great Britain
by Amazon